4th Edition, May 2006

FATIMA
IN LUCIA'S OWN WORDS

SISTER LUCIA'S MEMOIRS

Volume II – 5th and 6th Memoirs

Edited by
Fr. Louis Kondor, SVD.

Translated by
Dominican Nuns of Perpetual Rosary (Fatima)
and
Dominican Nuns of Mosteiro de Santa Maria (Lisbon)

Secretariado dos Pastorinhos
Fátima – Portugal

Imprimatur,
Fatimae, Augusti 2004
✠ Seraphinus, Episc. Leir.-Fatimensis

ISBN 972-8524-04-8
Depósito Legal nº. 243 055/06

EDITOR'S PREFACE

The profound and rapid changes to which human beings are being subjected affect each one of us both in the way we think and in the way we behave. They also affect the ways in which communities and social groupings of all kinds relate to one another. The communications media penetrate right into our homes with the greatest of ease, confronting us with all kinds of happenings, and spreading all kinds of ideas and sentiments. "Socialization" multiplies the various relationships that human beings have with one another and creates new bonds which do not always promote a person's full and healthy development.

As a result of all these changes, traditionally held values are frequently called into question, especially by the young, to such an extent that parents and educators find it increasingly difficult to fulfil their mission. Religious life itself has also been profoundly affected.

Faced with this situation, many voices from many quarters have begun to speak of a crisis of values in today's society. And the family is the human environment where this crisis is most acutely felt. The family had always been looked upon as the great channel through which principles, values and attitudes were handed on from one generation to the next... In our own day, however, the very institution of the family appears to be at risk.

Because the future of humankind lies with the family, which is the 'first and vital cell of society', it has been the object of a wide variety of campaigns. The Church, too, has a responsibility to discharge in this field. For this reason, Pope John Paul II gave a particalar emphasis to the celebration of the International Year of the Family with his magnificent "Letter to Families". Even before that, in 1981, he had given us the Apostolic Exhortation "Familiaris Consortio" which was the fruit of the Synod of Bishops on the Family. In it, he stressed the importance of marriage and of the family and the need for the Church to be involved. "Knowing that marriage and the family constitute one of the most precious of human values, the Church wishes to speak and offer her help to those who are already aware of the value of marriage and the family and seek to live it faithfully, to those who are uncertain and anxious and searching for the truth, and those who are unjustly impeded from living freely their family lives. Supporting the first, illuminating the second and assisting the others, the Church offers her services to every person who wonders about the destiny of marriage and the family" (no. I).

If the future of humanity depends on the family, and we can say the same of the family in relation to the evangelizing action of the Church, it is in the family, the "domestic church", that one has one's first experience of God. For this reason, the Pope goes on, "at a moment of history in which the family is the object of numerous forces that seek to destroy it or in some way to deform it, and aware that the well-being of society and her own good are intimately tied to the good of the family, the Church perceives in a more urgent and compelling way her mission of proclaiming to all people the plan of God for marriage and the family, ensuring their full vitality and human and Christian development, and thus contributing to the renewal of society and of the People of God" (no. 3).

The publication of this book can be seen as forming part of this dynamism. There are publications which pave the way for certain happenings, and there are others which are the fruit of such happenings. This one is a consequence of the International Year of the Family. Although urged by, and under obedience to her superiors, to some extent Sr Lucia wrote these Memoirs, in particular the one about her mother, under the impulse of this spirit of support for families. Her parents' home, which Sister Lucia inherited and gave to the Shrine in Fatima, has been transformed by those in charge of it into a place of pastoral reflection on the Family for the benefit of the pilgrims who visit it. The emphasis at Fatima is on the family. The Memoirs about her parents, "admirable examples of a Christian family, united in faith, hope and love" are, in a sense, a letter written by Sister Lucia to all who are concerned for the future of marriage and the family.

We wish to express our gratitude to Mons. Dr. Luciano Guerra, Rector of the Shrine, who took the initiative of persuading Sister Lucia to write these last two Memoirs, and who has now made them available for publication. We thank, too, Rev. Fr. Dr. Luciano Cristino and the Serviço de Estudos e Difusão do Santuário (SESDI) that he directs, for his kind collaboration in the preparation of the Introduction and notes, and in the correction of orthographical errors.

We thank Sister Lucia herself for the precious gift she has given to all families. Though written with love, the writing of it involved much sacrifice on her part, and for this we express to her our deep gratitude.

We also wish to thank the Dominican Nuns of the Pius XII Monastery in Fatima and of the Mosteiro de Santa Maria in Lisbon for their collaboration in the translation of the Fifth and Sixth Memoirs respectively.

We ask God that all who begin to read these Memoirs will end them in an atmosphere of prayer, making their own the words of Scripture with which Sister Lucia brings her Memoirs to an end:
"Give thanks worthily to the Lord,
and proclaim his wonders to the nations." (Tob. 13, 10).

Fr. Luis Kondor, SVD.

FIFTH MEMOIR

Introduction by Rev. Fr. Dr. Luciano Cristino

This text from Sister Lucia's hand which, in its literary genre, is similar to the Four Memoirs composed between the years 1935 and 1941 and already published, originated at the request of the Rev. Msgr. Luciano Guerra, Rector of the Sanctuary.

After the death on 26 August 1986 of Sister Lucia's eldest sister, Senhora Maria dos Anjos, who enjoyed the use of the house of her parents, António dos Santos and Maria Rosa, inherited by Sister Lucia, and donated by her to the Sanctuary, the office of the Rector undertook restoration work for the preservation of the building, to recall the epoch of the Apparitions and to serve as a place of pastoral reflection on the Family of today, for pilgrims to Fatima.

Besides the restoration of the house, care has been taken in the reconstitution of the furniture of the Apparitions period as far as possible, with its original objects, and in particular the ancient clock in the main room inherited by one daughter, Gloria and later by her daughter, Maria Rosa, presently residing in Brazil.

The Sanctuary also acquired the neighbouring house, which belonged to Lucia's godmother, Maria Rosa, transformed years ago into an Ethnographical museum, with the back garden and three properties attached, to be cultivated and arranged, so that the pilgrims could capture vividly the message of the second Apparition of the Angel.

The better to achieve this objective, Sister Lucia was asked to complete, in whatever way possible, the recollections of her childhood and the way of life in her family, namely in regard to her father

Sister Lucia responded with pleasure to this request, writing out, with her own hand, what can be called her Fifth Memoir. It begins with a letter addressed to the Rector of the Sanctuary, in the manner of a prologue, dated 12 February 1989, followed by a text dated the 23rd of the same month and year, and in conclusion, she adds a letter of the same date.

We publish these three documents, as they constitute a whole, while respecting as much as possible the original composition. We have simply checked the spelling, the accenting, the use of capitals or otherwise, the punctuation and the division into paragraphs. We have inserted some subtitles and explanatory notes.

After handing over this Fifth Memoir and its respective documents, Sister Lucia took the occasion to verify some point or other. We decided, therefore, to add the respective documents as an appendix.

1. Prologue

J.⁺ M.

To the Rector of the Sanctuary of Our Lady of Fatima

I received your letter, Reverend Father, dated 23 November 1988, in which you ask me to better describe the image of my father, since what I wrote in this regard in the Memoirs is so incomplete, and you wish to make our home a place of reflection about the family.

For this reason, I am willing, because I remember my parents as admirable examples of a Christian family, united in faith, hope and love.

It is true, that the picture I give in the Memoirs is very inadequate because I wrote amidst several difficulties – lack of time and of the necessary conditions to render it better by re-reading and correcting it. And, then, they were published without my previous knowledge. But what can be done? I offer my sacrifice to God, hoping that from everything, He may draw forth His own Glory.

In the same letter, Your Reverence asks insistently for a response to your questionnaire sent by means of our Provincial, Fr. Jeremias Carlos Vechina, and which was given to me by his Reverence on 31 October 1986 with the recommendation to respond as soon as it was possible.

Because, at the time, it was not possibe for me to undertake this work, I placed it in the bottom of a drawer, where it has remained until now.

Seeing that, Your Reverence had to come here on 14 April 1988, to deal with matters concerning the home of my parents, you renewed, with insistence, your request for a response to your questionnaire.

On 20 October 1988, our present Provincial, Fr. Pedro Lourenço Ferreira, at your request I think, advised me not to defer doing this work, believing it to be for the glory of God.

In view of all these insistent requests and recommendations, above all, those of my Superiors – in which I always see a sign of the will of God – I spoke about the matter with our Mother Prioress who considered it very carefully and decided to dispense me from assisting at some of the Community exercises, so that I would be able to dedicate the time to this work.

Therefore, believing this to be the will of God, and because it is what Your Reverence needs more speedily, I am going to begin by describing the portrait of my father, trusting in the maternal protection of Our Lady.

The responses to your questionnaire will be made afterwards, but, for now, I must say that to some – those referring to the Apparitions – I cannot reply without authorization from the Holy See, unless you would like to ask for this permission and obtain it. Otherwise, I will go ahead, leaving those questions blank.

I am going to begin the story about my father responding to question number 16 on your questionnaire.

And may God assist me, and may my father, who sees me from Heaven, take my hand again, as he did when I was a child, guiding it and teaching me to trace on my forehead the sign of the Redeeming Cross of Christ Our Saviour.

Coimbra, 12-2-1989

What I am going to say, in the beginning, is what I have heard from my parents, my godmother Teresa and other family members.

MY FATHER

2. Before the Apparitions

"Was there anyone thought to be rich in the village of Aljustrel? And why?"

Yes, there was the family 'Santos'. It was a large, Christian, practising Catholic family. They lived near the Family Ferreira Rosa, to whom the houses belonged and from whom the Sanctuary recently purchased, for a museum, the one which was my parents' – comprising the house, patio and kitchen-garden beyond the well. From there onwards, this family owned a great extension of properties in the direction of Montelo, Our Lady of Ortiga, Fatima, Valinhos, Cabeço, Charneca and Cova da Iria. My father was a member of this family and also Teresa Santos, my father's aunt. [1]

---

[1]   *Teresa de Jesus or dos Santos (1840-1929), was the paternal grand-aunt of Lucia, being the sister of Joachim dos Santos, father of António dos Santos.*

She lived, I'm not sure for how long, with her two unmarried brothers, [2] who, when they died, made her the heir of all their goods, thus she had two times more than the other brothers and sisters.

It was my father, who, while he lived, cultivated our lands together with hers, ploughing, sowing and reaping.

She employed three labourers and a maid called Inácia. [3] The men worked in the fields under my father's direction.

One of the servants was a young boy of 12 or 13 years of age.[4] He pastured a small flock of sheep which belonged to Aunt Teresa: some 15 or 20 sheep, like ours, all white and large, of the Merina breed, very productive of offspring, wool and milk. When my father required this boy to help with the field work, he ordered the two flocks combined and taken altogether to pasture. He ordered the same, when he had to plough some fields with grass, so that the two flocks, at the same time as they were grazing, would manure the land. On those days, the boy went to help in the field work, by walking ahead of the oxen as they ploughed, cutting the grass and gathering the food for the animals. Upon returning home at night, the two flocks of sheep caused no difficulty in being separated; because of their instinct for the water which they had in their troughs and for their own food, each one ran to their own pen, chewing the cud through the night, so that on the following day they gave better and more abundant milk.

Aunt Teresa afterwards married one of the workmen, Anastácio Vieira. [5] He was a very good friend of my father's and thus they continued, always sharing between the two of them, the farming tasks that had to be done.

They had no children. When I was born, my father invited Uncle Anastacio to be my godfather at Baptism, something he and my Aunt Teresa accepted with great pleasure. They asked my par-

---

[2] *José and Manuel dos Santos, born 14 June 1842 and on 23 January 1847 respectively.*

[3] *A maid named Inácia appears in the home of Teresa de Jesus and her husband Anastacio Vieira, on the roll of those confessed in the Parish of Fatima from 1907 until 1919.*

[4] *Perhaps Manuel Vieira, who appears as a servant in the home on the roll of those confessed from 1915 until 1919.*

[5] *They were married 29 November 1882.*

ents to give me to them, so they could bring me up as their own child and adopt me, but this my parents did not want. However, they did allow them to take me to their home whenever they wished, which happened frequently, always with the hope of fulfilling their desire. My godmother Teresa said that it was also to relieve my mother, who, in her charity, was at this time raising a little orphan, who had been left without a mother at birth.

Inspite of the Santos family being of a peaceable nature and the Ferreira Rosa family being of a more expansive type, playing the harmonium and the guitar, arranging *festas* and dances – this still persisted during my childhood, and I referred to it slightly in the Memoirs – various members of the Santos family married those of the Ferreira Rosa family; among them my father and his sister Olympia, who became the mother of the Servants of God, Francisco and Jacinta Marto.

Aunt Olympia in her first marriage, became the wife of my mother's brother, José Ferreira Rosa, [6] who, after having been in Mozambique, returned from there, bringing sufficient savings to allow him to restore the home of his parents, giving it the form that it has today, and to build for himself, when he married Aunt Olympia, the home where the Servants of God, Francisco and Jacinta Marto were born. He died eight years after the marriage, [7] leaving as heirs to his home and other possessions, his young wife, who received half and his two orphaned children, Antonio and Manuel dos Santos Ferreria Rosa, who received the other half.

The Ferreira Rosa family distinguished itself by the practice of charity. My mother's aunt, Maria Isabel Ferreira (Rosa) [8] taught children to read in the house which the Sanctuary eventually purchased as a museum. It must have been with her that my mother learned to read; my sister Teresa and my brother Manuel could also read and write well enough, likewise the children of Uncle

---

[6] *Son of Joachim Ferreira and Rosa of the Incarnation. The wedding was in Fatima Church, on 6 February 1888.*

[7] *On 10 September 1895, in Aljustrel. He was born on 19 October 1850, in the place called Perulheira, then part of the Parish of Reguengo and at present of S. Mamede.*

[8] *Maria Isabel Ferreira (†24-04-1890, 80 years of age, unmarried). Cf. Sixth Memoir, note 4.*

José Ferreira Rosa, António and Manuel. [9] She was unable to teach the other nieces and nephews, who were younger, perhaps because of illness. I did not know her, but I heard her spoken of with the deepest affection, esteem and veneration, especially by my mother. When I was very small, we still had an old wooden chest in our *casarona*, [10] where, it was said, my great-grandmother [11] hid her when, during the French invasion, General Junot wished to kidnap her. [12] This aunt of my mother, gathered abandoned children to care for them and afterwards place them in the homes of good families who would love them and help them through life.

[9]   The sister Teresa was born in 1893 and the brother Manuel in 1895, the cousins Antonio and Manuel were born in 1889 and 1895 respectively; so that only her mother, born in 1869, could have been taught by Maria Isabel, who died in 1890.
[10] A storage shed attached to the dwelling where various things were put away. In Sister Lucia's family home, this storage space was located near the kitchen.
[11] The mother of Maria Isabel Ferreira, also named Maria Isabel, was the great-great-grandmother of Lucia and not the great-grandmother.
[12] According to tradition, which was told to us by a cousin of Sister Lucia, Maria Isabel was very beautiful. "When Junot set up camp in Fatima, he made his general headquarters in one of the homes of the Santos Family. It's the ground floor and first floor of that house which is opposite the house of Jacinta and Francisco, and is close to the street. Junot invited our ancestor Maria Isabel to his table. Before appearing she blackened herself with soot all over. Junot respected her and compelled the troops to respect her also. When he raised camp, the general ordered the troops to get Maria Isabel in order to take her to France. The troops looked for her, but in vain. Seeing the great danger, her mother had hidden her in an old chest in the store house with lots of sacks on top. It is told that Junot looked upon Maria Isabel as a daughter."
      We do not know the date of Maria Isabel Ferreira's birth, once the Registry books of Baptisms and Weddings of Fatima, prior to 1810, disappeared around the third French invasion (1810-1811). The oldest books would already have been entered into the archives of the completed books of the Ecclesiastical See of Leiria, where they were burned. The more recent ones up to 1810, in use at the Parish, were mislaid, with the exception of a book of deaths which commenced in 1803. If the 80 years, recorded in the registry of death of Maria Isabel, which occurred on 24 April 1890, is correct, she was not yet born, at the time of the invasion of Junot (1807-1808). Of the other brothers and sisters, the ones of whom we have the approximate date of their births, Manuel was born around 1789, and died in 1884 at the age of 95 years, and Maria was born around 1802, since she was three years old when she died in 1805. But although there may be some error, through omission, about the age of Maria Isabel, it's not likely that the episode – if it is true – actually

She died unmarried, in the home of my grandparents, which afterwards my mother inherited. From my parents, I became the heir of this home and had the pleasure of donating it to Our Lady for Her Sanctuary of Fatima, in the hope that it may be for the glory of God, of Our Lady and the spiritual happiness of our pilgrim brothers and sisters who go there and enjoy seeing things as they were in former times. I believe that it was due to this aunt of mine, that it became the custom for the children of the region to come to play on our patio, together with me, and that the mothers came to leave their smallest children while they went about their different tasks. I have already referred to this in the Memoirs.

My father loved to see the children in our house, and, when it happened that he was at home, he amused them by telling them stories and playing with them.

My father was very diligent about taking his children to the Baptismal font. One day, I heard my mother speaking to Dr. Formigão in an interview. He was asking her about the date of my birth. My mother answered:

"We say that it is on the 22nd of March, because she was registered as having been born on that day, but, in fact, this is not the case. She was born on the 28th of March 1907. It was Holy Thursday; in the morning, I went to Holy Mass and received Holy Communion, thinking I would return in the afternoon to visit the Blessed Sacrament, but it was not to be, since on that afternoon, she was born. (Only then did I know the actual day of my birth. This is really not surprising, because in Fatima, at that time, no one attached any importance to one's birthday, it was not a feast; therefore, it was not something of which we spoke.) Meanwhile, as she

happened to her nor in the manner in which it was narrated. Some other episode during the third invasion could have happened, with some official of Massena, in which the occupation of the Diocese of Leiria, between 3 Octcober 1810 and 10 March 1811, left a trail of death. In the Parish of Fatima alone, of the 1147 inhabitants and 291 homes extant in the beginning of 1810, there were only 734 and 209 respectively at the end of June of 1811, 389 persons having died as a result of illness and 24 deaths by the French (cf. "mortality caused by the French invasion in the Diocese of Leiria", appendix to the Couseiro ou Memorias do Bispo de Leiria, Braga, 1868, pg. 362; Leiria, 1898, pg. 414; Leiria, 1981, pp. 304-306).

is registered as being born on the 22nd, we continue to say that this is her birthday. Her father made the arrangements for her Baptism immediately. It was not convenient for him the following week, because of his work, but, as it was required that the parents bring the children for Baptism on the eighth day after birth – otherwise they would have to pay a fine* – her father decided to give the date of her birth as the 22nd, so that the Parish Priest would baptize her on Holy Saturday, which was the 30th of the same month."

He invited, as godmother for my baptism, a young neighbor, a goddaughter of my mother. [13] She was happy to accept and went to ask permission of her father. It was the custom in those times, that young girls could not take any responsibility without their parents' permission. Her father asked her what name they were going to give to the child. She told him it was Maria Rosa, because the mother already had four daughters and none of them had this name, which was hers; she was also called Maria Rosa and an infant, who had preceded me, whom God had already taken to Heaven, had been named Maria Rosa. [14] Her father responded:

"No! You must name her Lucia! If that is not so, I will not permit you to be the godmother". [15]

She went to tell my parents who were surprised and asked:

---

*   *Required by the Civil Registry (Translator's note)*
[13]   *Maria Rosa, goddaughter of Lucia's mother, was the daughter of José Pedro Marto (brother of the father of the Seers Francisco and Jacinta) and of Maria Antonia. She lived opposite the house of Lucia's parents.*
[14]   *Maria Rosa, Lucia's mother, in the official inquiry made in 1923, said that "I had seven children, one having died at birth" (Episcopal Archives of Leiria, Documentos de Fatima, 1-6, fl. 10). Lucia as well as her sister Carolina de Jesus said that the child who died, at birth, was a girl. Manuel dos Santos, brother of Lucia, told Fr. Joaquim Maria Alonso, in 1963, that it was in fact a boy. His parents were going in a cart to a farm called Estrumeira da Conceição and, at the exit to Casa Velha, the cart turned over. Maria Rosa, who was pregnant, returned home immediately and gave birth to a stillborn child (unedited note of Fr. Alonso, in the Archives of the Sanctuary of Fatima). Perhaps he had been baptized conditionally or baptized at home. But the Baptism was not recorded in the book of the list of Baptisms. This fact took place between 1903 and 1906.*
[15]   *Carolina de Jesus told us that it was also José Pedro Marto who chose the name for her Baptism, as he was the husband of the godmother, Maria Antonia. Her godfather was the same as Lucia's, Anastácio Vieira.*

"But where did your father get such a name?"

However, out of courtesy, they agreed that I should be named Lucia. Thus, by the grace of God, I was baptized on Holy Saturday, 30th of March 1907, when the bells of the Parish Church announced the Resurrection of the Lord. [16] (At that time there was no civil register, it was only in the Parish Church).

My father was of a calm nature, kindly and joyful; he liked music, *festas* and dances. So that, even though the Santos family was of a different nature, he adapted very well to the ways of the Ferreira Rosa family .

He had no disputes with anyone, neither with the family nor with strangers. He loved to please everyone and to see everyone happy. For example, that little patch of land with fig trees, within our grounds, going toward the well, and which the Sanctuary purchased, it was my father who gave it to a certain family, because they lamented not having a fig tree near their home from which to gather figs to eat.

Neither my father nor my mother wished that any poor person should go away from our door without something. If my father was at home, it was he who gave; if not he it was my mother; if it was neither one or the other, it was the oldest son or daughter who would give the alms. To me – as the youngest – it happened often, because my sisters, in order not to interrupt their work, would send me, and this made me very happy. And, what was it that we gave? Sometimes, a handful of potatoes; other times, a bowl of kidney beans or of chick peas; other times a little olive oil was poured into the small jars that they carried; or even a piece of bread with sheep's cheese or a bowl of sweet olives for them to eat. At times, my mother, when she went to the salting-board to fetch the meat for the family meal, would bring something extra, and put it in the drawer of the kitchen table, folded in a cabbage leaf, and say:

"Leave this here; it's for the first poor beggar who appears, asking for alms."

Whenever there was meat left from the family meal, my mother placed it between two slices of bread, and put it on a small earthenware plate in the drawer, saying:

[16] *Civil Registry of Ourem, Registos Paroquiais de Fátima, Baptismos, 1907, n.º 31, fls. 5-5 v.º*

"Leave this here; it's for the first poor person who comes along, asking for alms."

I recall here what happened one day: my father was at home, sitting on the steps of a stairway which led to the attic, shelling beans. My mother was seated opposite, leaning against the corner of firewood, peeling potatoes. I was still very small, so I was playing outside on the patio, which was closed by a large gate made of wooden slats. I saw near the gateway a poor beggar asking for alms. I ran into the house and said to my father:

"There's a poor man outside begging for alms."

My father got up, went to the fireplace, and with his pen-knife cut the string of black pudding (they were hanging up to dry) and holding it in his hand, he asked my mother:

"Look here, may I give this to that poor man? Do we need it?"

My mother replied:

"Yes, you can. What we give to the poor has never left us in need."

My father, very pleased, went out to the gate to give the pudding to the poor man. Seeing it, he raised his hands and prayed an Our Father and a Hail Mary. While the poor man prayed, my father remained in front of him, standing, with his head uncovered. When the beggar finished, he said:

"May the Lord grant good fortune to you and to your little girl."

My father answered:

"Good-bye, my brother, until the next time!"

And he went into the house again. I ran after my father and said to my mother:

"The poor man prayed for father and for me, so that God may give us good fortune."

My mother replied:

"And for me, nothing?"

I did not know what to say. Then my father said:

"For you also, because you and I are one; everything that is mine is yours and our children's."

My mother responded with a smile:

"Then it's alright!"

And the two of them remained in their humble work and friendly conversation, while I returned to the patio to play and watch for any more beggars who might come asking for alms.

Certainly, at the time, I did not understand the full meaning of this event, but it made an impression on me and I did not forget it. Today, however, I understand its great moral and spiritual value.

Often, at nightfall, the poor came asking for a place to rest. We always gave them somewhere to lie down. We shared our supper with them; they prayed grace after meals with us which my father intoned and then the Rosary, if it was a day on which it was prayed. Afterwards, during the winter, while my mother tidied the kitchen, my sisters worked on the loom and at the sewing, while my brother foddered the animals, giving them the final rations of the day. My father used to cut the chestnuts and sweet acorns, putting them on the embers to roast, so they could be eaten at nightfall while they worked to the sound of the guitars, of the fados, and popular songs and ballads of lengthy verses, which the poor folk sang if they happened to be blind.

Or, if it was summertime, we went to the threshing floor, where there was always something to do: if it was not the day for husking, then, it was peeling, by moonlight and by the light of the lanterns hanging on the poles nearby, the broad-beans, peas, kidney beans, chick-peas or lupin, which were kept for seed and sifting the seeds from the cabbages, lettuces, turnips, etc , all the while taking in the cool air which was so refreshing.

Our house was like a house for everyone: it had a door where all knocked and at which all were attended. Sometimes they came to ask if we had any bread, so that we might lend them one or two loaves, because they had finished theirs and it was not yet the day for baking a new batch. My mother always had some:

"Go and take it, it' s there! "

In the summer, they came to ask for pitchers of water, because their wells and cisterns were dry, and to go and fetch it at the new spring was so far away... My mother, and my father, if he happened to be at home, would always say yes, giving them the key to the cover of the well (my parents always kept the well closed with an iron padlock, so that no insects, animals, or children, who were playing there, would fall in) saying:

"Go there and fill your pitchers."

And God blessed it, because the water of our well never failed.

Other times they came to ask if we had any onions left which we could spare, because theirs had run out and those of the new harvest were still very small and it was a pity to gather them so early.

"Go ahead, to the baking room and take what you need," answered my mother, or my father, if he was home.

My parents had them hanging on string from beams of wood on the roof of the baking room. And so it went on...

Thus all were our friends and we were friends who were at the service of all.

One day, my sister Maria dos Anjos said to my mother:

"Why do you bake such large batches of bread? Afterwards, we don't eat it all and it just gets hard!"

My mother replied:

"So that we have some over to give those who come to ask; and later on, whatever is left can be cut into slices, toasted in the oven and used in the 'weary-horse soup', * or fried, so that everyone has enough to eat."

Frequently, they came to ask my mother if she would go to their homes because someone was ill. My mother left everything and went, leaving whatever had to be done to any of my older sisters, who were at home.

I recall one day, on which my godmother Teresa was in our house, talking with my mother. A small boy came, the son of my Aunt Prazeres [17] – theirs was the first house on the left side of our home, going toward Casa Velha – to ask my mother if she would go to his house, because his mother was ill. My mother quickly got up to go. My godmother Teresa told her:

"Well, my dear, you'll wear yourself out, wanting to attend to everyone!"

My mother replied:

"Never mind, I help others and God helps me."

If it happened to be at night that they came to call my mother, it was my father who got up to go and help. Afterwards, he brought the message to my mother and, while she was dressing, he lit the lantern, so that she would not stumble or fall along the way.

---

* A mixture of bread, sugar and wine guaranteed to revive even the most exhausted. (Translator's note)

[17] Maria dos Prazeres, wife of Manuel Gonçalves da Silva.

When the influenza epidemic came in 1918, only my parents, my brother Manuel, my sister Gloria and I were at home. It seems to me that my sister Carolina was in Leiria. [18] The epidemic struck almost all the people. My mother and my sister Gloria went, from house to house, caring for the sick. One day, my uncle Ti Marto warned my father that he should not permit my mother or his daughters to go to the homes of the sick to treat them, because it was an epidemic which was contagious and we might also get sick.

That evening, upon arriving home, my father forbid my mother and his daughters to go to the homes of the sick to treat them. My mother listened, in silence, to all that my father said and then responded:

"Look, you have a good point. It's just as you say. But, look here, how can we leave those people to die, without anyone there to give them a glass of water? It would be better if you came with me to see how these people really are, and, then, if it's alright to leave them alone."

And, pointing to a large pot which she had hanging on a chain from the chimney, over the fire in the fireplace, she said:

"Do you see that pot? It's full of chickens. Some are not ours; I brought them from the homes of the sick because ours were not enough for everyone. They're cooking in order to make a broth, and I have over there all ready, the small pots which I brought from their homes, in which to carry them. If you would like to come with me, you could help carry the baskets with the pots of broth and, at the same time, you will be able to see for yourself and then we can decide what has to be done."

My father agreed. They filled the pots with broth and they went out together, each one with two baskets, one in each hand. A little

[18] *Carolina de Jesus told us, at that time, she was not in Leiria but in the locality of Ramila, as a servant. When her sister Teresa, who was married in the neighbouring place of Lomba, fell sick, Carolina was called to take care of her niece Maria Julia, born on 26 February 1918. When the two ladies of Ramila who nursed the little girl, became ill, Carolina took her to Aljustrel, where she found that all the people were sick. Carolina's stay in Leiria was much later. She was working as a servant in Terreiro, in the home of Julio Pinto, who had a commercial establishment on the Rua Direita. Lucia went with her mother to visit her sister, on 16 June 1921, around the time of her departure for the college of Vilar, in Porto.*

later, my father returned with a baby in a little baby-basket and said to my sister Gloria and to me:

"Take care of this child. The parents are both in bed with fever and are not able to look after him."

He went out again, and a little later returned with two more children, who were already able to walk, but still could not care for themselves, and he said:

"Take care of these two also, they do nothing but cry at their parents' bedside, and they both have fever and are not able to care for them."

And so he brought more. I don't remember how many.

The next day, they came to say that in my Aunt Olympia's house also, they were all in bed with the fever. My parents went there also to care for them. Then, in time, everyone got better, but four of them always remained with some traces of the fever which weakened them and, one after the other, in a few years, these four died: Francisco,[19] Jacinta,[20] Florinda,[21] and Teresa.[22]

In those days my parents did nothing except go from house to house, to treat the sick. My father and my brother Manuel also cared for the animals that were in their pens bleating with hunger, and they brought the milk to give to the sick and the children. To these they also gave soups made of softened bread in chicken broth; to the older ones, minced meat in the chicken broth, with rice, and the same was given to the sick who were getting better.

The need was so great, that my parents did not hesitate to allow me to go to spend, some nights, in the home of a widow who lived alone with her son, who was in the last stages of Tuberculosis. In this way, she would be able to rest, knowing that she had an eleven year old girl there, who could take a glass of water or a bowl of broth to her son, or who would call her if he should need something else.

I don't remember the name of this woman or of her son, but I do recall the house. It was between the home of my Aunt Olympia and the blacksmith's. In order to enter, one had to climb a stone

---

[19] *He died on 4 April 1919.*
[20] *She died on 20 February 1920.*
[21] *She died on 7 May 1920.*
[22] *She died on 3 July 1921.*

stairway which led from the street. The young patient, spent the night sitting in bed, propped up on pillows struggling to breathe. At times, I went to the kitchen to fetch the fan and waved it before his face, to try to give him a little air. When he saw me there, he was so pleased, that he would say that those were the best nights he spent.

Some people also warned my father that it was foolish to allow me to go to that house because I might catch the disease. My father replied:

"God will not repay me with evil for the good that I do for Him!"

And so it happened! My father's trust was not confounded, because today I am almost 82 years old and yet I have not felt even the slightest trace of that disease!

One day, I heard a conversation which my mother was having with the Father Vicar of Olival [23] who asked her about my father. My mother said:

"He was always a good Christian, practising Catholic and a good worker, even as a youth. Therefore, I liked him very much and we were married. He was always very faithful to his religious duties and to his state, and a very good friend to me and the children. When I told him that God was going to grant us a seventh child, he responded:

"Don't be troubled! It is one more blessing from God. Therefore, there will be no lack of bread in the drawer nor oil in the pot."

On Sundays and Holy Days of obligation, my father went with the whole family to assist at Holy Mass – almost always at the midday Mass. We rested a little longer in the morning, took care of the animals, put the house in order, left the dinner prepared, and went all together, well rested, and without pre-occupations.

When I was still very small, my father carried me in his arms or seated on his shoulder. When we arrived at Church, he handed me to my mother, because, at that time, the men were separated from the women in the choir and in the sanctuary. On returning, after Mass, he likewise came home with the family. My older sisters went in front, each one speaking with her fiancé who waited for them in the churchyard; my parents were the last couple, who followed

---

[23] *Fr. Faustino José Jacinto Ferreira (1835-1924), Parish Priest of Olival, district of Ourem, from 1886, and Vicar of the Vicariate of Ourem, from 1892.*

behind, talking also with my godfather Anastacio, my godmother Teresa, my uncles and the other people who joined them, and along the way, they bid us farewell at their own homes, saying: "Good-bye, till we meet again!"

The others continued on their way and, upon arriving at our house, they said good-bye with the same "Adeus" and proceeded further on. It was the same for my sister's friends: they bid fare-well, to return later on at mid-afternoon, to continue their conversations.

We entered the house, ate our dinner, and, while my mother and some of my sisters tidied the kitchen, the others and my brother took care of the animals. If it was good weather, my father sat on a stone bench, which was on the patio, at the kitchen doorway, playing cards and talking with my uncles and the others; my sisters dispersed in pairs, to the shade of the fig trees, talking with their fiancés; my mother, with my godmother Teresa, aunts and other neighbors, sat on the small steps which we climbed from the side of the road to enter our house. While some rocked their babies to sleep, they were, at the same time, conversing and watching their older children, who were playing on the road, running up and down, amusing themselves with their children's games and, at times, imitating the processions which they had seen, singing the Litanies of the Saints, etc.

At sunset, when the bells of the Church rang for the Angelus, my father got up and, with him, all the others. Removing his cap, my father led the three Hail Mary's to which they responded. Then, quite content, they said good-bye, each one going to his own home to have their evening meal and rest. For they had spent the Lord's Day well in His grace, having fulfilled His Law, and were thus ready to carry on with their labours the following day.

And the friends of my sisters and the other young girls who came there left also, some passing over the serra in the direction of the hamlets; others, walking along the paths in the direction of Santa Catarina, passing near the Cova da Iria, which, at that time, was no more than a deserted field. There maize and potatoes grew in the hollow, with olive trees on the slope, which produced a fine olive oil, the holm-oak trees which bore the sweet acorns for both men and animals; the strawberry-tree which produced berries, used for making *aguardente (a home-made potent liquor)*; hay and grass, food for the animals and the brushwood, for the farmyard pens. And they went along paths yet further away, playing their harmoniums and guitars, singing and hoping to return on the following Sunday.

After supper, my father intoned the thanksgiving, prayed the Rosary – for it was not a day on which we did evening work – and went to rest, since at dawn of the following day he would have to rise early, in order to resume his weekday work.

My father and my brother were the ones who slaughtered the pigs of my godfather Anastacio and ours also; singeing them, washing them and hanging them to drain off, until the next day. Afterwards, they broke them into sections, cutting the meat into pieces, leaving separated, in earthenware pans, those which were to be placed on the salting board, those which were to be made into sausages, those to be consumed fresh, and that which was to be shared with the people who had none. Those to whom it was given included: the Parish Priest; also a little old man who lived alone in a tiny house close to the house of my Aunt Olympia, the mother of Jacinta; [24] another, a lame and crippled man, who also lived alone, three houses away, on the left hand side going toward Fatima; an old woman, who also lived alone in a small house next to the blacksmith's shop on the left side, coming towards our house and the widow of Uncle Agostinho,[25] who also lived alone, since the death of her husband. I was then sent to take our little gift to these people.

[24] *Anastacio Pereira, who died on 13 November 1934 at the age of 81 years. He had another brother Francisco, who died on 22 April 1919, at the age of 60 years. They were both unmarried.*

[25] *Josefa de Jesus, widow of Agostinho de S. José who died 13 October 1912. Carolina de Jesus related to us a childhood event, which actually occurred at the time of the death of Agostinho. When Senhora Maria Rosa was teaching Christian doctrine in her home to her children and to the other children, she asked them, on a certain occasion, after having explained about the Three Persons of the Most Holy Trinity: "Who died?" And little Lucia answered triumphantly: "It was Ti Agostinho!" In fact, the correct answer that the children ought to have given, under pain of not passing the examination by the Parish Priest, was: "It was the Son because He took a body like ours, and thus He was able to suffer and to die."*

There was a small, white wicker-basket in our house, in which my father told me I had come from heaven with flowers. It was only used when they dressed me as a little angel, to walk in the processions carrying it with flowers, to strew before Our Lord, and also to carry our gifts to the poor and to our friends.

On Christmas Eve, after supper, while we waited until it was time to go to Midnight Mass, we stayed near the fire-place, making the *filhoses*.* While my mother and my sisters stretched out the dough and laid it flat in the boiling oil, my father, with a large iron fork, would turn them over and remove them to an earthenware pan, placing them inside a sieve to drain.

At the precise time, we went to midnight Mass, bringing the wicker-basket with the gift of the *filhoses* that I carried up to the Infant Jesus, when I went to venerate His image after Mass,** and again, on Christmas morning, to the persons mentioned above.

Our flock was, usually, of some 20 or 30 sheep. In the Spring, they doubled, or even tripled, because many of the sheep had double offspring. My father killed the male lambs for food for the family, and used the milk for breakfast and making cheese. The ewes were allowed to be nourished and to grow, but, as soon as they began to eat, they were separated, in order to use the milk for the same purpose. And, when they had grown large, my father chose the best to provide continuity to the flock and those left over, with the older and tired sheep, he sold.

It was my father who killed the foxes, hares, genets and rabbits which he hunted with skill, placing the traps on the large flat stones; he skinned them and prepared them for my mother to cook; he hung the skins on the branches of the fig tree, so they could be sold to the mule drivers who would be passing by.

When the bells of the Parish Church rang out the evening Angelus, my father stopped his work. Removing his cap, he prayed the three Hail Mary's and came home. While he waited for supper

---

*   *Filhoses are very old, traditional fried pastry cakes which are prepared especially at Christmas time in Portugal. (Translator's note)*
**   *There is a custom in Portugal of allowing the faithful to come forward to venerate – to kiss – the image of the Infant Jesus held by the Priest celebrant after the Christmas Masses. This custom is still practised. (Translator's note)*

– if it was good weather (if it was not, he waited near the hearth)– he sat on a stone bench which was on the patio, leaning against the wall of the kitchen with me on his knees. He amused himself by telling me stories, and teaching me to sing local songs, fados, and popular songs of ten stanzas or four line verses, etc. My mother was there at her work. From time to time she came over to us and said:

"What are you teaching this little one! If only you would teach her doctrine!"

Then my father would say:

"Let's do as your mother wishes!"

And he took hold of my little hand, teaching me to trace the Sign of the Cross on my forehead, mouth and heart. Afterwards he would teach me to pray the Our Father, Hail Mary, the Creed, how to prepare for Confession, the Act of Contrition, the Commandments of God, etc. Later on, when we were all together at supper, he made me repeat what I had just learned and, quite content, he turned to my mother and said:

"Do you see? It was I who taught her."

My mother replied smiling :

"You are indeed a very good man! May you always be so!"

My father answered:

"God has given me the best woman in the world!"

This is what made me believe that my mother was the best in the world and, when the other children came to our patio to play with me, I used to ask them:

"Is your mother good? My mother is the best in the world!"

Sometimes in the evening, he took me to the threshing-floor and we sat down on the stone seats, to enjoy the cool breeze, which was so pleasant there. And then, pointing to Heaven, he would say to me:

"Look, up above, it's Our Lady and the Angels: the moon is the lamp of Our Lady, the stars are the lamps of the Angels, which they and Our Lady light and place in the windows of Heaven, in order to light up our way at night. The sun, which you see come up, every day, over there, at the back of the serra, is Our Lord's lamp which He lights every day to keep us warm and so that we can see in order to do our work. Because of this, I used to tell the other children that the moon was Our Lady's lamp, the stars the lamps of the Angels and the sun the lamp of Our Lord.

There on the threshing-floor, he continued to teach me the truths of the faith, to sing and to dance. From time to time, my mother and my older sisters – those who were at home – came to peep through the branches of the fig trees and, laughing, they would say:

"She looks like a little spinning top, with her tiny arms in the air, trying to imitate all the movements she sees father making."

And my mother would come, with a cup of refreshment made of honey prepared with cool water taken from the well at the last moment, so that my father could drink it with his little spinning top. And she also, sat down at my father's side, talking joyfully and laughing, feeling so content.

My father also used to tell me, that, when there was a thunderstorm, it was Our Heavenly Father scolding men because of their sins .

One day, my father was working near the well. I was there playing near him. Suddenly, the weather began to grow dark, to thunder and rain. My father threw down the hoe, grasped hold of me and ran to the house. Once at home, I asked him:

"It's Our Heavenly Father scolding someone. Who has sinned, was it you, father, or someone else?"

My father responded:

"It was I and others also . Let's pray to St. Barbara, to deliver us from the thunder and lightning!"

And he knelt down with my mother and my older sisters who were at home, in front of a crucifix which was on the wall of the outside room, to pray Our Father's and Hail Mary's.

On rainy days, when he was unable to go to the fields to work, my father was at home, where he would cut the firewood to the exact size needed for use in the oven and the fireplace, and then put it in stacks on the patio to dry. Afterwards he put it away in the shed, and in the oven room, in order to keep it dry so that it would burn without smoking.

On the days on which my mother was baking bread, if he happened to be at home, he helped her to put the wood in the oven. When it was hot, he took the ashes outside, cleaned the oven and, while my mother moulded the bread, he placed it with a baking-shovel into the oven to bake.

If my sister Maria dos Anjos had a lot of work, he sat at the weaver's shuttle filling the spools for the loom.

If he saw my mother carrying the pitchers, he took them from her hand and went to the well to fetch the water. He did the same with the pails of food for the animals, taking it to them and looking after them.

My mother said that, when the new babies were born and they cried during the night, it was my father who got up to attend to them and carried them to her bed so she could give them a little milk without having to get up herself.

One day, I went to the rabbit burrow, I caught a tiny rabbit and took it outside to play with it on the patio, but I did not hold on to it very well and the little rabbit ran away from me. I went to tell my mother and she scolded me, saying I was naughty and disobedient, because she had told me many times already that I was not to go to the rabbit burrow. Then I asked:

"You say that I am bad, father says that I came from Heaven in a wicker basket with flowers. So then, are there bad things in Heaven also?"

My mother replied:

"Well, yes, the demons were angels who were in Heaven but, because they were bad, God put them out, and now they go about tempting everyone. As for you, He sent you here below to see if you'll be good, so as to be able to return there."

And I replied:

"But I don't remember!"

"Of course not," responded my mother, "because you were asleep and you are very forgetful."

That night, when my father came home, I told him what my mother had said to me and he replied:

"Very well, but don't be worried! That's for when you are older; as for now, you are very small. Therefore, you still have a lot of time to become good."

It seems that he guessed rightly, because I am nearly 82 years old and still going along here, in the hope of being good in order to go to Heaven. But, as Jesus Christ has said that only God is Good, He will have to take me there, in His mercy, without waiting for me to be good.

I just finished revealing – with deep emotion – what I was able to recall of the life of my father, in the bosom of his family, approximately up to the time of the Apparitions.

By that time, more or less, my two older sisters had married and left home to go and set up their own homes.[26] With this, our house was like a desert. The young girls who came to learn weaving and sewing, stopped coming, because my sisters who used to teach them were no longer there. The children who came to our patio to play with me, also did not come anymore, because I spent the day in the field with my sheep. Only a small group of neighbours came to wait for me, as evening fell, in order to spend the last hours of daylight together with me, and, on our threshing floor, to watch for Our Lady and the Angels to come to light their lamps and place them in the windows of Heaven, to light up the way for us.

That marvellous threshing floor – which they tell me has been destroyed – how I wish that Father Rector would order it restored, not only as a remembrance of my parents, where they enjoyed the fresh air of the serene summer nights, teaching me to raise my eyes to Heaven, where Our Lord is, Our Lady and the Angels who watch over us and help us on our paths through life, but, also, for the children of that time, especially, the Servants of God Francisco and Jacinta Marto, who used to run there to join me, waiting, and watching for when our heavenly Mother would come with the little Angels to light their lamps and place them in the windows of Heaven, to light the way for us.

It is true, this is a child's perception, but it teaches us to lift our gaze to Heaven, where we know that God Our Father is, the Blessed Mother whom He gave us and watches over us, and the Angels that He created and destined to guide us and lead us on the paths of life.

3. During the Apparitions

The Apparitions came to pass. While my mother was so distressed, my father maintained an attitude of faith and trust. When

---

[26] *Maria dos Anjos was married on 23 August 1916 to António dos Santos (Valinho) and went to live in a house opposite the house of her parents. Teresa de Jesus was married on 14 February 1917 to José Pereira and went to live in Lomba.*

my mother became even more upset, judging everything to be a hoax, my father said:

"Don't be upset! We do not know if it is true, but we also do not know if it is a lie. Let's wait and see."

When he saw the harvest lost in the Cova da Iria, he said:

"For this year all is lost, but, in October, if the Lady stops coming, the people will stop going there also, and we can return to cultivate it as before."

When, after the Apparitions, he saw that the people continued to go there, and the property was lost, he said:

"If it was Our Lady who appeared there, she will help us get along without the Cova da Iria."

Also, during the Apparitions – it must have been towards the end of July – one day, as evening fell, my father arrived home, called me and said:

"Come with me for a walk to the well."

And so we went. Arriving there, he sat on the edge of the well, made me sit at his side and said to me:

"Look, now you're going to tell me the truth, whether you saw that Lady in the Cova da Iria or not. Don't be afraid to say that you didn't see her, or if you said that for a joke and right away all the people believed – or simply, that you lied. There are many persons in the world who tell lies; don't be afraid to say so if you did. Then the people will stop going to the Cova da Iria and everything will be finished."

I answered:

"I know. But if I saw, how can I say that I did not see? And the Lady says to continue to come every month, until October."

My father got up and we went home.

The next day, after supper my father said to me:

"While your mother and your sisters straighten the kitchen, you come along with me to the threshing floor."

We went. My father sat on one of the stone seats that was there, made me sit at his side, and said to me:

"Tomorrow morning, very early, you go with the sheep to the Cova da Iria. I'm going with you."

I replied:

"I'm just sorry for Jacinta, because I'm sure her mother will not let her go so early."

My father answered:

"That's not so important. Go and tell Aunt Olympia that, very early tomorrow morning, you are going with our sheep to the Cova da Iria. Jacinta and Francisco, if they wish, can go there later. Tell her that you are going there early because it is so far away and that you want to come home earlier because of the heat; and that if people come wanting to speak to you, your mother will tell them to go there to find you, since your sisters are very busy and cannot go and take your place."

I went to give the message to my Aunt, who answered:

"Very well; but for now, say nothing to Jacinta, so she'll not be crying. I'll tell her in the morning."

On the following day, my father called me very early in the morning. I got up, and we had our breakfast, while my mother took the milk from the sheep, then we went out by way of the wasteland, so as to avoid meeting people along the way. We could hardly see. When we arrived at the Cova da Iria, the first sign of daybreak began to appear behind the serra, in the direction of Aljustrel.

We crossed over the road and descended the slope, between the olive trees, guiding the sheep along the narrow way in a zig-zag fashion – since one could not descend straight down – to the Cova. There my father saw that, indeed, everything had been trampled on and eaten by the animals. From the crop sown that year, which was corn, no profit at all would be gained. And he said:

"We've lost twenty measures of grain, along with the kidney beans and the pumpkins which were planted in between. Patience!"

We left the sheep in the Cova, to take advantage of the grass which still remained on the edges, and we climbed the hillside in front, along side the great holm-oak tree. On top, behind the spot where one now finds the Basilica, there was a piece of flat land, with some holm-oak and olive trees, between which my father used to sow, in alternating years, wheat, chick-peas or rye, etc. There, things were not so spoiled but the tips of the trees were already eaten away by the animals, just like those on the hillside. My father saw this and said:

"Indeed, we can expect no harvest from here. But, there may be some olives, acorns and berries which escape up above, on the tree tops." He saw the little stone wall that we were making when we saw the reflection of light from Our Lady – which we thought was lightning – and we descended the slope by the side of the large holm-oak tree, at the front of which, a little below, was the small holm-oak where Our Lady appeared. My father approached it, looked at it and asked:

"Is it here that the Lady appears?"

"Yes, it is," I replied.

"How many more times is the Lady to come?"

"Until October," I answered.

"If the Lady does not return afterwards, the people will also stop coming and, next year, we will return to cultivate the Cova da Iria as before."

And he asked:

"What do the people come here to do?"

I replied:

"They come to pray the Rosary and they all want me to pray with them."

"Well now," said my father, "you pray the Rosary with me also."

"Yes, I will pray."

My father knelt with me before the little holm-oak tree and we prayed the Rosary. When we finished, my father got up and said:

"Now you stay here with the sheep. I'm going to see your brother who is working on the moorland. When the day begins to get too hot, you are to go home with the sheep."

And I remained alone – I don't know if I cried – in that lonely field, where I heard only the tinkling of the sheep bells, the chirping of the little birds hopping on the tree-tops and the crowing of the cocks in the Moita hen-houses.

By mid-morning, two groups of people arrived there. The first one came from the direction of Moita and Santa Catarina. Hardly had I finished praying the Rosary with this group, when another appeared, coming from Montelo and from the direction of Minde. I prayed another Rosary with them also. And then, with my sheep, I went home, since the heat was already so intense.

My father also came home to eat supper. Afterwards, he told my mother all that he had seen. For that year, he told her, we could count on nothing from the Cova da Iria; everything was destroyed. But he continued:

"If it is Our Lady who appears there, She will help us!"

My mother replied:

"Our Lady?! If only it was Our Lady! Who can tell us that it's Our Lady? Not at all! It's evil, it's the devil who has come into our home. We were so happy and now we cannot get rid of all these people, constantly knocking on the door, wanting to see and speak with our little girl; and unless we go and fetch her, they won't go away. If at least you would come home, you could help send them away."

"But," my father answered, "I don't know what to say to them and I cannot be rude to them, by sending them away from here. So, that's why I don't come."

It happened that, many people took advantage of the evening, at the end of the day's work, to come to our house, in order to find out what was going on. I don't know, but perhaps my mother may not have been completely mistaken, that, partly, it could also have been the devil who was furious and wished to hinder the good which the Message came to bring to the world.

What cost my father more and made him avoid being there, instead of coming home at night as soon as he had finished his work, as was his custom, was to find the house continually invaded by strangers, asking impertinent, curious and even – very often – misleading questions, from which he did not know how to get away.

A few days before the 13th of August, Ti Marto and my father were notified to appear at the Administration Office of Vila Nova de Ourem, with their children. My uncle, Ti Marto said:

"I'm not taking my children. I'm not going to bring such small children before a tribunal."

My father said:

"I'm taking my daughter, because I understand nothing about these things."

The following morning, in the company of Ti Marto, he took me to Vila Nova de Ourem. My father and Ti Marto went on foot. I went riding on the back of a donkey, from which I fell about three times, not because I was not used to riding but because I was falling asleep, due to the sound of my father and Ti Marto conversing and of the slow, easy-going pace of the donkey. But the falls did not hurt me because I only tumbled down towards the front. And my father came running to set me once again on top of the donkey and to exhort me to be careful not to fall.

At the office of the Administration, the Administrator questioned my father and my uncle Ti Marto, to whom was given a strong rebuke for not having brought his children, as he had been told to do. He questioned me also, wanting me to tell him the secret. Seeing that he couldn't get anything from me, he dismissed us and in the afternoon we returned home.

At home, my father, always serene and tranquil, recounted to my mother and the family what had happened. He only said:

"I lost a day's work because of this. Patience! If it is Our Lady who appears, she will help us."

It was a sign of his unfailing confidence in the protection of Our Lady. He showed the same trust, when, some days later, they took us, Francisco, Jacinta and myself, as prisoners to Vila Nova de Ourém. My father said:

"I am not worried about them; they cannot do any harm to children of that age. And if it is Our Lady who appears to them, she will protect them."

On the 13th of October, because the rumour was spreading that, at the moment of the apparitions in the Cova da Iria, they were going to throw a bomb and that we would all die there, my parents, for the first and last time, wished to accompany me, saying:

"If she is going to die, we want to die also at her side."

And they left the house with me, but, on the way, I lost sight of them, amidst the multitude of people who crowded around me.*

4. After the Apparitions

When, after the Apparitions, my father began to see that the people, instead of ceasing to go there – as he hoped – went more and more in greater numbers, transforming that site into a sacred place, of faith, prayer and penance where pilgrimages were flocking in the spirit of faith and confidence in the maternal protection of the Mother of God, he said:

---

* "That is, my mother, for my father managed to break through the crowd and take me by the hand up to the little holm-oak tree." (*Author's note in Letter of 16 April 1989*)

"We've lost the Cova da Iria forever. We can no longer count on the produce of that land but, if it is the work of God, He will help us to get along without it."

When they came to say that the people were leaving money near the little holm-oak tree where Our Lady had appeared, which was gathered up and left for him in compensation for the loss of the land, he said:

"God forbid that I should keep this money! It doesn't belong to me. It belongs to Our Lady! Neither do I want anyone in my family to keep as much as five pennies of that money! As for the loss of the land, it is Our Lady who will repay me and she will help us."

It was thus that Senhora Maria Carreira –who got the name of 'Ti Maria da Capelinha'– began to keep the money so that it would not be stolen.

Later on, they went to ask my father's permission to build a little Chapel of Apparitions (Capelinha). He not only gave the authorization, he wanted to contribute, giving for that purpose twenty square metres* of land with a strip of land for access from the road to the site of the Capelinha. He thought, in the beginning, of putting up an iron fence as a barrier, which the people could not cross over, thus allowing him to continue to cultivate the land which remained. But, then, he realized that the multitudes could not be held back, and therefore, it was useless.

The number of persons flowing continually to our home, wishing to see me and to speak with me, was greater than ever. My mother did not know what to do! She discussed the situation with my father, to see what solution they could find. She was not able to go constantly to the field to fetch me, nor did she have anyone to send to take my place, and the people would not go away without my coming to attend to them and to go to the Cova da Iria to pray the Rosary with them. And people from every part came, from far and near, rich and poor, priests, learned and simple people from the villages, many with their sick who were so pitiful! My father suggested selling the sheep. My mother replied:

"I already thought of that. But, how can we get along without the products of the sheep? The wool that we use here at home and

---

* I meant to say: Therefore, he gave a square piece of land, 20m. long and 20m. wide. (*Author's note*)

that which we sell, the pigs which are killed each year for the sustenance of the family, the hogs and sheep which are sold to help with the expenses of the house, the milk and the cheese! And now we no longer have the produce of the Cova da Iria! How can we manage wíithout all that?" *

My father responded:

"Perhaps, with what we cultivate in those other fields, we might be able to make up what we have lost here and there. We can try; if afterwards, we find that we cannot make ends meet without the sheep, we can buy them again. And the little one could start going to school – the first school for girls had just been opened in Fatima – and you can tell those who come wishing to see her and speak with her, that she is in school and that they can find her there; then the teacher may do as she thinks best, and you will feel relieved. God will help us! As many sacrifices as we make, we will never be able to repay God for the grace of sparing us from the influenza epidemic which did not enter our home, nor did He allow any of the children who were here during those days to become ill."

Because of the fuss that there was in the village against the Parish Priest, in which my father did not wish to be involved, but which left him with a very bad impression, he stopped making his Easter duty, as was his custom, and kept away from the Parish Priest, no longer confessing to him. But he did not stay away from Church; he continued to go to Holy Mass every Sunday and on Holy Days. He went, instead, to Vila Nova de Ourem for confession, and each year he went to confession and Holy Communion for the Feast of Our Lady of Ortiga, in order to gain the jubilee indulgence. He went there in the last year of his life, and took me with him, a few days before his death. Afterwards, we went to supper at the home of my sister Teresa, who lived near there, in a place called Lomba. And she hardly expected that it would be the last time she would be speaking to our father or see him alive! And

---

* When, in the Memoirs, I say: "Because we had already lost some of the lands, the means of subsistance began to grow scarce in our house", I wished to refer to the loss of the Cova da Iria and the lack of the sheep products. My explanation was very incomplete, due to lack of time and the conditions conducive to re-reading and correcting it. (*Author's note*)

so it is, this mortal life, in which we find ourselves... It disappears like smoke which vanishes in the air.

Happily, my father accomplished well his mission on earth.

He fell sick on 30 July 1919. My mother called for the doctor who diagnosed it as a case of double pneumonia. He prescribed treatment, but the medicines were of no avail. On the following morning, feeling somewhat worse, my father asked my mother if she would send for the priest, to make his confession and receive the last Sacraments. My mother warned him that, very likely, she would only be able to find the Parish Priest.

"Don't worry about that!" answered my father, "it doesn't matter, as long as it's a priest!"

My mother sent for the priest, but the Parish Priest delayed, thinking it was not an urgent case, and my father died in the arms of my mother and of his sister Olympia, repeating the ejaculations which they were suggesting to him and which were used at that time in such cases:

"Jesus, Mary, Joseph save my soul which belongs to you!"; "Lord Jesus, have mercy on me, by the merits of Your Life, Passion and Death on the Cross!"; "Father, into Your hands I commend my spirit!"

Thus, I feel entirely at peace, with respect to the eternal salvation of my father, certain that the Lord received his beautiful soul, into the arms of His infinite Mercy and presented him into the full possession of the immense Being of God, our Father.

As I write this, I am recalling the story of King David, who – inspite of having been such a great sinner – was chosen by God, to have among his descendants, St. Joseph, Our Lady and Jesus Christ, Son of David – Hossana, to the Son of David! – The One Who said He had come to save sinners, because it is not the healthy who need the doctor, but, indeed, it is the sick.

Coimbra 23-2-1989

Sister Maria Lucia

J + M

To Rev. Fr. Luciano Guerra
Rector of the Sanctuary of Our Lady of Fatima

Pax Christi

In response to the letter of Your Reverence of 23 November 1988, I am sending the description of what – with the deepest sentiments – I could recall about my father. I hope that something will be of use in fulfilling the wishes of Your Reverence.

With regard to the clock, which was in my parents' home, I received a letter from my niece Maria Rosa, who is living in Brazil, saying that she already gave it to her sister Preciosa, who also lives in Brazil. She is thinking of coming here next Summer in order to bring it. They say that the casement is not the same anymore because their mother –my sister Gloria– seeing that the original one was so old, substituted it for another which she ordered to be made. It's a pity but now there is nothing to be done.

I also have three objects –very small– which were from our home. I don't know if they interest you. If so, I have already asked permission to give them to you. One is the *Imitation of Christ* which my mother sent to me at Porto when I was in school there, along with another book from which she used to read to us. But this one, the Superior did not give me. She told me that in school I could not read it, that she would give it to me when I left, but until today... I suppose that it could have been the *Missão Abreviada*, by the appearance and being a book with which I was already familiar, but as I only saw it in the hands of the Superior and did not see the title, I cannot be sure. The *Imitation of Christ* I have always carried with me. It is now very old, but it's the same one.

The other two objects are: two crochet needles, those with which my mother taught me when I was still a child. One is made of metal and I used it to make lace for underclothing. The other is of bone, which I used for making woolen garments for warmth in winter. Jacinta began to work with these, because she wanted to learn and so I taught her. And very soon, she was making the narrow lace quite well. The needle made of bone has no large hook now but I worked with the small one up until a short time ago. I have always kept these with me, as a remembrance of my mother and of Jacinta, but as there are many of these here in the house, if I should need one, I won't miss them.

That is all for today. In union of prayers.

Coimbra, 23-2-1989

Sr. Maria Lucia

APPENDIX TO THE FIFTH MEMOIR

In the letter accompanying this Fifth Memoir, Sister Lucia referred to the clock in the living room of her parents' home, a copy of the Imitation of Christ, and two crochet needles which she intended to offer to the Sanctuary of Fatima.

The Rector of the Sanctuary, in thanking Sister Lucia for the Fifth Memoir, on 13 March 1989, told her that he was pleased "because Sister Lucia has used the style of the previous Memoirs, recounting above all concrete events, kept in her memory and in her heart." He was also pleased about some details regarding the threshing floor, which is going to be restored, the information about the clock, to be put back in its place, and about the three objects already referred to: "they interest us very much, since all these personal keepsakes, stir up in the pilgrims sentiments which, at times, go very deep, even to the very depths of which only the Lord knows."

In fact, these articles, as well as the clock offered by Sister Lucia's niece Maria Rosa Vieira were given to the Sanctuary for the purpose intended.

The Rector of the Sanctuary announced further, that he was going to carry out the plan for the arrangement of the back garden and the house of Sister Lucia, in order to enrich the Family Pastoral theme, and of the house which belonged to her godmother, which was converted into a museum and which would be joined to Sister Lucia's, in the same design, without losing its purpose as a museum.

Sister Lucia, upon offering the book and the needles mentioned above, wrote:

J. ⁺M.

To the Rector of the Sanctuary of Our Lady of Fatima

Pax Christi

The two crochet needles included here are the ones with which my mother and my two older sisters, Maria and Teresa, taught me to crochet, when I was still a child.

With the metal one, the Servant of God, Jacinta also learned. Seated near me, she saw me crocheting and asked me to teach her, and while I was working with the needle made of bone, making woollen garments, I loaned her the metal one and taught her to make narrow lace to decorate underclothing, which she was able to do quite well.

I have always carried them and kept them with me, as a remembrance of my mother and of my childhood, along with the *Imitation of Christ*, which my mother sent to Porto for me when I was in school there.

It is with love and devotion that I now, –with the permission of our Mother Prioress– detach myself from these three humble objects and offer them to Our Lady for Her Sanctuary of Fatima, to place in the house belonging to my parents and which today is Hers, for the glory of God and joy of our pilgrim brothers and sisters. May they always give praise and glory to God and to Our Lady.

Coimbra, 15-3-1989

Sr. Lucia

To a remark made by the Rector of the Sanctuary, regarding the propriety of Sister Lucia's adding, in this Memoir, a reference to the crisis which her father passed through, at a particular time, "though understanding that she would do this within the context of the filial devotion, which she has towards her father and which is only proper", Sister Lucia responded in this way:

J. + M.

To the Rector of the Sanctuary of Our Lady of Fatima

Pax Christi

I beg your pardon since I am only now responding to your letter of 16 March 1989. Time did not allow me to do otherwise.

As to your note in reference to what I have written about my father, in the last period of his life, Your Reverence says: "Since you made reference to the crisis which your father passed through, people may consider that it would be well to refer to that crisis in this Memoir."

I always try – as much as possible – not to repeat what I have already said elsewhere in order to save time and to avoid what seems unnecessary to me.

Thus, the content of the last manuscript seemed to me sufficient to explain and complete the statement in the Memoirs, since the result had seemed to be so inadequate.

Despite the great mystery of human weakness, my father never went to excess, to the point of losing his balance, nor failing in the awareness of his duties as a Christian and practising Catholic, always maintaining the dignity of his personality as head and father of the family, faithful to his matrimonial promises, friend of his wife and children, preserving peace and serenity in his home.

Finally, I recall the holy King David who, inspite of having been so great a sinner, because he repented, did penance and changed his life, was chosen by God so that from among his descendents would be born St. Joseph, Our Lady and Jesus Christ, the Son of God.

Thus, I believe that what counts more in the sight of God is not so much the sin as the humble repentance with which we ask pardon along with the sincere intention of never again offending the Lord.

In this regard, I am remembering what St. Irenaeus tells us: "It is in the weakness of man that God manifests His power." Yes, only God is great and powerful, above all in His merciful love! To Him be our gratitude, praise and love.

Because of your letter, I re-read the manuscript about my father and verified that, on page 20, paragraph 6, it would be well to add, at the end of the sentence, a note to clarify the meaning of what I say there: "That is, my mother, for my father managed to break through the crowd and take me by the hand up to the little holmoak tree."

And may God help us with the maternal protection of the Immaculate Heart of Mary.

Coimbra, 16-4-1989

Sr. Lucia

This explanation of Sister Lucia along with a letter written by her, dated 10 December 1951, which was published in 'Voz de Fatima', were thought sufficient for the above-mentioned addition to the 5th Memoir, for this reason we publish here also the letter referred to:

J + M

Carmelo of St. Teresa, Coimbra, 10-12-1951

To His Excellency The Bishop (*D. José Alves Correia da Silva*)

I am grateful for the two letters of Your Excellency, the first of which crossed with one of my own. I received also pictures of Jacinta and the cloth for the relics. As soon as they are ready, I shall send them as you wish and, if Your Excellency desires more, you have only to send us the pictures, on which we put the relic, and we will send them back. We usually put the seal of our Order on the back with its emblem. I do not know if Your Excellency has one of the Diocese or of the Sanctuary. If you have and prefer that we use that one, in your kindness could you please send it to us.

Now, Your Excellency, I ask your permission to clarify something that seems to me necessary for the glory of God.

Some have spoken to me of a film, which was being spread, I believe in Portugal, Spain and America, and according to what they have told me, the picture they give of my father is false and, besides being false, it is not edifying to souls, nor for the glory of God. According to what was told to me, they picture my father miserably intoxicated, selling the Cova da Iria bit by bit, greedily running away with the bag of money etc. etc. Now, nothing of this is true. Your Excellency and the priests appointed by you at the Sanctuary know very well that my father not only sold absolutely nothing of the Cova da Iria, but, neither he nor his wife nor any of his daughters nor his son, kept anything at all of the money which the people left in their faith near the holm-oak tree, and this, in spite of being on his land, which, from the time of the Apparitions was rendered useless for producing anything, making what, until then was cultivated there, a grave loss to the family sustenance. To a rich family, this would not have been a great loss, but to the poor even a little is a big loss.

As for the drinking, again thanks be to God, it was not as they say, nor as Fr. De Marchi wrote in the first edition of his book, *A Lady More Brilliant than the Sun*.* If my father did sometimes drink

---

* *The original title of Fr. De Marchi's book, which is currently published under the title, Fatima From the Beginning. (Translator's note)*

a little more than those who drank nothing, he never carried it to the point of creating disorder at home, nor of ill-treating his wife and children. He was a sincere and honest man and, although he died within 24 hours of double pneumonia, he left his family neither weighed down in debt nor with the burden of any troublesome business. If it is true that some years passed without his having made his Easter duty in the Parish, because of a disagreement that he had with the Parish Priest, he did not stop going every year, to Our Lady of Ortiga, on her feastday and there he confessed and received Holy Communion in order to gain the jubilee indulgence. And he said that he did this because there he could choose another confessor instead of the Parish Priest and he did not have to go to the Sacristy to recite his doctrine.

Even in the last year of his life, he went there and took me with him, and after receiving Holy Communion went to eat at the home of my sister Teresa, who was already married and living in a nearby place, called Lomba.

He also went to Mass on Sundays. Usually, he carried me with him and, when we arrived at the Church he climbed the steps to the choir, where the men assisted at Mass, and sent me to join my mother who was in the body of the Church, with the other women. It was after Mass, in the company of his friends, that he delayed longer coming home and, at night, when he came from work and went to give an account to my godfather Anastacio of how things were going in their fields (as he took care of both ours and theirs), he remained longer talking and in the tavern, and came home late; with that, my mother was very distressed, as she was so used to seeing him at home at suppertime and spending the evening cheerfully in the bosom of the family.

For my mother, in her uprightness of spirit, this was indeed a great fault. I have referred to this in one of the writings which you requested of me, but perhaps I did not know how to express myself very well.

The hard times our family went through just then, or at least the lack of former abundance was due to various things and circumstances, among them —and one of the principal causes— was the Apparitions. The Cova da Iria, as I said, left quite a need in our family's livelihood; moreover, it was my mother, and not my father as Dr. Walsh states erroneously in his book, who decided to sell the flock because of the many people who sought me and, who were so insistent in wanting to speak with me, that they were offended if they were not satisfied. It was for this reason, and not for any other that my mother sold the flock – because otherwise, one of my sisters would have to lose a day's work at home in order to replace me in the field – and the produce of the flock was also a great loss to the sustenance of the family.

It happened at this time also that my two older sisters married. One was a weaver and the other a seamstress and therefore, they had also helped very much with the income from their work. Added to all this, there was the great perplexity of my mother with regard to the Apparitions, which more than anything else was the cause of her trouble and lamentation.

Please excuse this explanation but I thought it was called for in the interests of justice and charity, and because of the veneration and respect in which I hold the memory of my father.

With gratitude to Your Excellency, I humbly and respectfully kiss your holy ring and ask your blessing. With the greatest respect and filial devotion,

Maria Lucia of the Immaculate Heart, I.C.D.

(Episcopal Archives of Leiria, Documentos de Fatima, B2-166, published partially in "Voz de Fatima", year 29, no. 353, of 13-2-1952, pg. 29, nº 353, of 13-2-1952, pg. 2, cols.3-4).

SIXTH MEMOIR

Introduction by Rev. Fr. Dr. Luciano Cristino

Some time after Sister Lucia had completed the Fifth Memoir about her father (first published in March 1990), Mons. Luciano Guerra, the Rector of the Shrine in Fatima, asked her to write one about her mother, even though her mother had, in fact, featured quite prominently in the first four Memoirs, and particularly in the Fourth, all of which had been written between the years 1935 and 1941.

This Sixth Memoir was begun in 1992 and completed on 25th March, 1993 but not actually delivered until 28th June, 1993.

In transcribing the text, we have followed the same procedure as in the case of the previous memoirs, respecting the original as much as possible. We have simply corrected or added in italics (in curved brackets) occasional words that had been misused or omitted by mistake; we have also placed in brackets some words used wrongly (in normal script). * We have also corrected the spelling, the use of accents and capital letters, and punctuation. We have also included in full the less common abbreviations.

In the dialogue sections, we have kept to the form already used in the other Memoirs.

We have inserted some sub-titles and explanatory notes.

* It has not been possible to show where these amendments occur in this English translation. Moreover, in order to clarify the meaning for English-speaking readers, it has occasionally been found necessary to add one or more words [in square brackets].

MY FATHER'S HOUSE, THE LAND WHERE I WAS BORN

My father's house, the land where I was born,
Arms of the mother that rocked me.
God knows how much I suffered for you
And you for me in fervent prayer,
Life goes on but the heart does not forget.

You were mother and you were guide,
Mistress and Lady, tree of life,
Chosen by God to be united with you
In the steep climb
Up the Redeeming Hill.

He knows why He chose us,
And his gaze bestowed upon us
Torrents of grace, light and life,
On the steep slope of his Calvary.

But now you are in Heaven, you see God unveiled
In the grace of his encounter
Thank him for the daughter He gave you
And pray for her until you see her with you in Heaven.

If only I alone
Could have carried the cross that He gave us,
But God chose to give you to me
Like another Simon of Cyrene.

On this radiant day of grace and light,
All doubts dispelled, do not forget me,
Until God chooses to call me to your side,
When there will be sweet kisses and tender embraces,
In the undying light of God.

MY MOTHER

1. Prologue

In the name of the Father, of the Son and of the Holy Spirit –
Ave Maria!

Since I wrote the Fifth Memoir about my father, various people
have asked me to write about my mother too, as they felt that her
virtue deserved to be made known, for the glory of God and as an
example of Christian life as a wife, mother of a family and housewife, always punctilious and industrious in the performance of her
duty towards God, the members of her household and those outside it. The Commandments of God's Law were her rule of life.
She inculcated these into everyone, with special reference to what
Jesus Christ says to us in his Gospel. «When a young man who
approached Our Lord asked him: "Master, what good deed must I
do to have eternal life?" Jesus replied: "Why do you ask me about
what is good? One there is who is good. If you would enter life,
keep the commandments." "Which?" the young man asked. Jesus
replied: "You shall not kill; you shall not commit adultery: you shall
not steal; you shall not bear false witness; honour your father and
your mother; and then you shall love your neighbour as yourself."»
(Mt. 19, 16-19).
A lawyer, too, questioned Jesus, asking him which was the
greatest commandment of the Law. Jesus gave him this reply: "You
shall love the Lord your God with all your heart and all your soul,
and with all your mind. This is the greatest and the first commandment. The second is like it: You shall love your neighbour as yourself. On these two commandments depend all the law and the proph-
ets" (Mt. 22, 37-40).

What I propose to write about my mother will show how she
had these precepts engraved in her heart and her mind. It was as
if God had said to her what he said to Moses so that he, in turn
could communicate it to the people: «Hear, O Israel! The Lord our
God is one Lord! You shall love the Lord your God with all your
heart, with all your soul and with all your might. And these words
which I command you this day shall be upon your heart. You shall

teach them diligently to your children, and shall talk of them when you sit in your house, and when you walk by the way, and when you lie down and when you rise. And you shall bind them as a sign upon your hand and they shall be as frontlets between your eyes. And you shall write them on the doorposts of your house and on your gates» (Dt. 6, 4-9).

My mother may well not have known this text of Sacred Scripture as I have reproduced it here, but she seemed to have it engraved in her heart and mind. Thus she carried it out and taught her children and her acquaintances to do likewise.

During Lent, after supper, she used to teach the catechism to the whole family, including, sometimes, the young people who came to our house and often stayed the night as they had come from a distance. She would begin by saying: "Now we'd better see if we remember our catechism, otherwise we shall be put to shame when the time comes to fulfil our Easter duty". Then she began with the Ten Commandments of God. She would say the words first: "First, to love God above all things. This is the one that confuses me most because I never know whether I love God more than my husband and children, but God is so good that He will forgive me and have mercy on me". And she would go on, listing all the commandments. When she came to the sixth, which requires us to be chaste, she would stop again and say: "We have to be very careful about this, too, because there are many temptations and many dangers. And you" turning to my brother and sisters "must be very careful not to let yourselves be deceived, nor have any dealings with anyone who suggests such things to you. The grace of God first and foremost, [then] our good name, our own personal honour and dignity. God gave me the grace of offering Him the pure flower of my chastity on the day I was married, when I placed it on His altar and received, in exchange, other flowers, namely the new lives which He wanted to give me. In this way, God has helped me and blessed me." And then she would go on, reciting, after the Commandments of God, those of the Church, the theological virtues, the works of mercy, and so on, as they were printed and taught in the catechism book that was used in those days.

Then it was my father's turn, then that of my brother and my sisters, one after another according to age, and finally it was my own turn, being the youngest. Sometimes my father would say:

"She doesn't need to, as she hasn't yet made her First Communion."

But my mother would reply :

"Yes, she does, because the parish priest puts her standing on top of the cupboard in the sacristy and asks her the questions to which the others don't know the answers, so she has to have it all on the tip of her tongue."

And I would listen to, and repeat, everything, parrot-fashion, without understanding the words or the meaning. Nevertheless, they were being absorbed by my spirit and stored in my memory, so much so that today I remember them with an intense longing for those happy times when innocence takes in and stores up everything as happy memories for later times.

The Law of God and of his Church were the bedrock of my mother's great virtue, a fact which those who knew her and had dealings with her well knew how to appreciate and admire.

Once, when Dr José Galamba de Oliveira was speaking to me in Valença do Minho about my mother, he said to me: "You know, your mother is more like a woman of Old Testament times than a woman of today".

Fr João De Marchi, in his book *Fatima from the Beginning*, said: "She was all that a woman should be: worth her weight in gold; she had tact, and intelligence".

One day, the then parish priest of Fatima, Fr Manuel Marques Ferreira, was asking me questions in front of a group of priests. One of them, the Vicar of Torres Novas, in an attempt to make excuses for some faults for which the parish priest was reprimanding me, started to ask him questions about my mother. The parish priest replied: "Her mother? Her mother is a saint!" (*Fatima in Lucia's own words,* 11th English edition, page 88).

Thus, backed up by the testimony of such respectable people who knew her and had had dealings with her, I, too, venture to say – not in the way the Church does when it declares that someone is a saint, but in the ordinary sense in which the word is commonly used, when one wants to show the very high opinion one has of the virtue and good qualities of a person with whom one has lived – in this sense I too say: "My mother was a saint!" She was humble, a woman of great faith, who loved justice and truth, was full of

charity, and was always ready to help people both in the household and outside it.

My father used to say that my mother was the best woman
in the world : "God gave me the best wife in the world!" (*Fifth
Memoir p. 25).*

I do not mean to say by this that my mother really was the best
wife in the world. Apart from Our Lady, with whom there is no
comparison, many other women have been good and holy. Some
of them have been canonised as saints by the Church, while the
names of others have gone with them into the silence of the tomb.
Nevertheless, in Heaven they are all sharing in the glory of the
immense Being of God. St. Irenaeus says that man alive is the
glory of God, and the life of man is the vision of God. This is what
matters most : to possess eternal life in the presence of God and in
the possession of his immense Being.

I hope that God, in his great mercy, has already granted to my
parents this great grace, and that, from there, already in full possession of the Truth, they will help me to undertake this task, too,
for the glory of God; and that my mother will again take my hand —
as she used to take it when, as a little girl, she held me on her lap
and took my hand to make me make the sign of the redeeming
Cross of God our Saviour on my forehead — and help me to guide
the pen to write on the paper what God wants me to record of the
times when I had the happiness of living with her and receiving
from her such wonderful teaching, such good and affectionate
example, always inspired by a living faith, hope and love.

Thus, it is with the help of her whom God gave me as mother
on earth as well as with the maternal protection of Our Lady that I
shall try to undertake this task, too, in the hope that it will be for the
glory of God, and trusting in the help of His grace that it will be a
moral incentive, for all those who will read the humble lines I am
writing, to keep going on the way of more faith, greater hope and
more intense love until it pleases God to transfer us from earth to
Heaven and cause us to rise again from the dust of the grave –like
a fresh young plant bearing flowers and fruit, growing up out of the
dust of the seed in the earth– in order to establish the new earth
and the new heavens with the multitude of the elect.

This work will also, I think, be the best means of fulfilling the
request of the Rector of the Shrine in Fatima that I should not leave

unrecorded any detail of what I remember of the life of our family, assuring me that it is for the glory of God and Our Lady. So I believe and so I hope, trusting also in the assistance of the Holy Spirit.

As I have already spoken about my mother in various other places, especially in the Fifth Memoir, because, as my father used to say "you and I are one", it is quite impossible for me to speak of one without speaking of the other; hence, here too, this is (what) is going to happen.

2. The Ferreira Rosa Family[1]

When I wrote the Fifth Memoir about my father, I wanted to give an idea of what our family life was like, and what I wrote there seemed to me sufficient. But Fr Rector has asked me to describe everything that I remember. In order to comply with this request, I am going to write all that I remember about my mother in order to give as detailed an account as I can of the life of the family in which it pleased God to give me the gift of life.

It was a large family of practising Catholics. Ferreira Rosa was the family name, and my mother was a daughter of this family which lived in Aljustrel, in the parish of Fatima. Next door lived the Santos family, to which my father belonged.

The family owned land and lived in the house with a kitchen garden and a well that are very familiar to many people today.

My maternal grandfather, my mother's father, was a native of Aljustrel, Fatima, and a member of the Ferreira Rosa family. I have already spoken about him in the Fifth Memoir that I wrote about my father.

This grandfather was born on 29th November, 1823, and was baptised and given the names Joaquim Ferreira Rosa, on 7th December of the same year.

He married, in Perulheira, a young woman called Rosa da Encarnação, a native of Perulheira, where she had been born on 21st April, 1825.

---

[1] Many of Sister Lucia's family dates were obtained chiefly by consulting the parish registers, before and after 1911; they were supplied by one of her cousins.

They were married in the parish church of Nossa Senhora dos Remédios in Reguengo do Fetal. They settled in Perulheira and their Christian home was blessed by God with the following seven children:

MANUEL, who was born on 28th October, 1846, and was baptised on 8th November of the same year.

He became a policeman in Leiria, where he married a young woman whose surname was Varela – I don't remember her first name as we always called her 'Aunt Varela' *(Maria José)*. They had two children. One of these was a little boy whom I never knew as he died as a baby; the other was a daughter called Laura Varela Ferreira Rosa, whom I knew well because her parents, my uncle and aunt, used to ask my parents to allow me to go to their house as a companion for their daughter, a request that my parents agreed to from time to time. She was a dressmaker, and my uncle and aunt wanted me to learn with her so that we could work together, but in the end my father did not agree to this.

My cousin Laura had cousins surnamed Varela on her mother's side. They lived in a house almost opposite that of my uncle and aunt and were also great friends of mine, playing with me and giving me presents. Among other things, they gave me a gold chain to wear round my neck with a gold medal in the shape of the letters that make up the words "God protect you". The older of these two cousins, whose name was Maria Emilia Varela, married in Lisbon. When Fr Joaquim Maria Alonso was doing research before writing his critique, he interviewed her, too. My cousin Laura never married and died in Lisbon.

JOSÉ was born on 13th October, 1850, and was baptised on October 20th. He emigrated to Brazil, but the ship was sunk. He managed to save himself by clinging to a piece of wood, all the time imploring the help of Our Lady of the Rosary. Eventually he was picked up by an English steamer which took him to Mozambique, where he worked for a number of years and then returned to Aljustrel, where his parents –my grandparents– were still living. He brought with him enough money to repair and restore his parents' house, giving it the appearance it has today. It was in this house that I was born. He also built the house, where the Venerable Francisco and Jacinta Marto were later born, at the time of his marriage to Aunt Olímpia, my father's sister. It was here that he established his Christian household and it was there that he died on 10th September 1895, leaving a young widow, my Aunt Olímpia, and two young sons, António and Manuel. Aunt Olímpia inherited half of the house and other property; the two boys inheriting the other half.

His grandchildren now include two Salesian Fathers, Fr Júlio, who worked for many years as a missionary in Mozambique, and Fr José António, who is now parish priest of the parish of Nossa Senhora dos Prazeres in Lisbon. In addition, one of his granddaughters, Sister Florinda, is a Dorothean Sister.

Aunt Olímpia married again. Her second husband's name was Manuel Pedro Marto. They were married in the parish church in Fatima on 17th February, 1898. They had nine children. [2] Three must have died very young, as I only knew six of them: José, Florinda, Teresa, João, Francisco and Jacinta. The last two are the ones who are now known as the *Blessed* Little Shepherds of Fatima.

My maternal grandparents' third child, ANTÓNIO, was born on 26th February, 1853 and was baptised on 6th March, 1853. He married a young woman called Maria do Rosário, a native of Aljustrel, where António built a farmhouse for his Christian family which God blessed with many descendants, including a niece who is a Dorothean Sister.

The fourth child's name was JOAQUIM. He was born on 11th October 1855 and was baptised on the following 22nd October. He emigrated to Brazil. The last news that was had of him was from the General Mine Headquarters. He is known to have had many children and grandchildren, but they have not kept in touch.

My grandparents' fifth child was VITÓRIA. She was born on 14th April 1858 and was baptised on the following 25th April. She married José Moço in the parish church in Fatima, where the young couple built a house to which they moved on 31st October 1886.

---

[2] *There were only seven [not nine] children of Olímpia of Jesus' second marriage. Of these, there was only one that Lucia did not know,: the first little Teresa, who was born on 27th February 1901 and died on 11th October 1902.*

God blessed them with many descendants who are now living in many parts of the world: Lisbon, United States of America, Brazil, etc. She died in 1934.

My grandparents' sixth child was JUSTINA, who was born on 22nd January and baptised on 3rd February, 1861. She was married and settled in Perulheira. She died giving birth to her first child, a girl, to whom my mother was godmother; she also helped to bring her up. They called her Maria Rosa, and brought her to Aljustrel, and took care of until her father married again, when he came to fetch her. However, she often came and stayed for long periods with her maternal grandparents in Aljustrel. She used to say that my mother had been a second mother to her, that she had always helped her and supported her in the difficulties of life. She marred Joaquim Carreira Mariano, and they built a house for themselves in Casal Gil. God blessed their union with eight children: one died at birth, the other seven survived. They have many grandchildren who are now living in various parts of the world, such as Venezuela, Switzerland, France, etc. Many of the grandchildren did higher studies, others are in business; as far as I know all of them live good and well-ordered lives.

3 – Maria Rosa: from birth to marriage

The seventh child born to my maternal grandparents was MARIA ROSA, who, 38 years later, became my mother. She was born on 6th July, 1869, and was baptised on the following 18th July in the parish church of Nossa Senhora dos Remédios in Reguengo do Fetal, sub-district of Batalha, Diocese of Leiria.

I was struck by a detail of her baptismal certificate. Although it is quite common for Christian families to choose Our Lady as one of the godparents in the baptism of their children, in this case, this detail seems to me to have a special significance: might not God have wished in this way to place this particular child from her very cradle under the special protection of Our Lady, in order to protect her and prepare her for her close association with the Message which He would be sending to us 48 years later? In any case, everything has a place in God's plan.

I found my mother's baptismal certificate fascinating, because it was written in the old-fashioned style then in use, impregnated with a great spirit of faith and Marian devotion, and because it mentions Our Lady as godmother, so I thought it appropriate to reproduce the wording here :

My mother's baptismal certificate :

"On the eighteenth day of the month of June in the year one thousand eight hundred and sixty nine, in this Parish Church of Nossa Senhora dos Remédios in Reguengo do Fetal, sub-district of Batalha in the Diocese of Leiria, I solemnly baptised a female child to whom was given the name Maria, which had been born in this parish at seven o'clock in the morning on the sixth day of the month of July of the said year, legitimate daughter of Joaquim Ferreira, native of Aljustrel, in the parish of Fatima, sub-district of Villa Nova d'Ourem, and of Roza da Encarnação, native of Prulheira, who were married in this Parish Church of Nossa Senhora dos Remédios and are parishioners thereof, residing in Perulheira; [the child being] the grandchild on her father's side of José Ferreira and Justina Roza of Aljustrel, parish of Fatima, and on her mother's side of Manoel dos Reis and Maria Joaquina of Prulheira.

The godfather was Manoel Ferreira, brother, unmarried, and the godmother Maria José da Prulheira, representing Our Lady, housewife, all of whom I know to be the persons they claim to be. In witness whereof I made this entry in duplicate which I then read to, and corrected, in the presence of the godparents, who did not sign their names with mine. In witness whereof

Manoel Gomes Mendes, Parish Priest." [3]

There, in Perulheira, in her father's house, she was brought up and educated as a Christian by her parents, until my grand-father, at the request of an aunt and uncle, returned to Aljustrel, bringing his wife and family with him, with the exception of his daughter Justina who was already married and remained in Perulheira, as I have already mentioned.

I do not know exactly when my maternal grandparents moved to Aljustrel. We think it must have been in 1883 or 1884, because they left their daughter Justina behind, and she had been married on 5th February, 1883. My mother must have been 13 or 14 years old at the time.

---

[3] *Leiria District Archive – Parish Register – Reguengo do Fetal, Baptisms – Entry no. 24, fl. 22v-23.*

My grandparents and their family were welcomed with great celebrations and demonstrations of joy, not only by the uncle and aunt who had asked them to come, but also by all the inhabitants of Aljustrel and the surrounding villages.

They were very cheerful and willing to be of service, good singers and guitar players, sponsoring parties and dances, so they subsequently became very popular with all the young people of the district.

Aunt Isabel lived with one of her brothers [4]. Neither of them had married and they were both already old and ill. They were very happy to be surrounded by all those cheerful young people, who treated them with respect, dedication, affection and love.

My grandparents, with their children, dedicated themselves to cultivating the old people's fields, producing from them enough to keep the family as well as to care for the two old people, providing them with the best of everything that was to be had in those days. My grandmother and my mother nursed the couple devotedly.

I don't know exactly when my uncle, Manuel Maria Ferreira died [5]. Aunt Isabel died on 24th April, 1890, when my mother was 21. She must have lived with my aunt for 7 or 8 years. She used to speak about this aunt with immense longing, respect and affection. When I was little, we still had in our barn an old chest in which, according to my mother, Aunt Isabel's mother had hidden her at the time of the French invasion, when the General took a fancy to her as she was pretty and wanted to take her back to France with him [6].

This aunt used to dedicate herself to charitable works and she also taught children to read. I imagine it must have been she who taught my mother to read, and that the books that were in our house even in my time, some of them written in a very antiquated way with lots of [*letters that looked like*] «f's», had formerly belonged to

---

[4]   *Manuel Maria Ferreira (†18-12-1884, 94 years of age, unmarried) and Maria Isabel Ferreira (†24-04-1890, 80 years of age, unmarried), were the children of João Ferreira, a foundling of the Royal Hospital of Lisbon, and of Maria Isabel of Aljustrel, and they had several sisters and brothers, among them José Ferreira, one of the maternal great-grandfathers of Sister Lucia.*

[5]   *Manuel Maria Ferreira died on 18th December, 1884, aged 95. Cf. ibid.*

[6]   *Cf. Fifth Memoir, note 12.*

her. I think some of them were by Padre Afonso Rodrigues S.J. [7] because when, later on, I became a Dorothean Sister, we were normally required to make our spiritual reading from these books, and there I found many of the stories that I had heard when I was little. I gained little or nothing from what was read. Usually either my mother or my brother read, at night after supper in the wintertime, during extra work time when my sisters were either weaving or sewing. I myself was little and went to sleep, and my father would put me to bed.

When, later, I began to go to school and learnt to read, my mother used to ask me to do the reading. Then I would take hold of those books, but I did not understand what was written in them. I used to say to my mother that there were lots of mistakes in them and that I couldn't read them!

I don't know what happened to those books. Perhaps my brother, when he got married, took them with him because by that time my mother's sight was failing and she read very little.[8]

One of the books – I think it might have been the *Missão Abreviada* [9] – was sent to me in Porto by my mother, together with the *Imitation of Christ*. But the Superior of the college, who received them, only gave me the *Imitation of Christ;* she showed me the other one but kept it, telling me that while I remained at the school I could not read the other book and that she would give it to me when I left. As, afterwards, I entered the Congregation as a religious, I never saw it again, nor did I ask for it. [10]

I kept the *Imitation of Christ* until a short time ago. When I learnt that the Rector of the Shrine in Fatima was looking for objects that had been in my parent's house, with Mother Prioress'

---

[7] *"Exercícios de Perfeição e Virtudes Cristãs" is the book in question.*

[8] *The copy of this work that was in Lucia's parent's house may well be the one that is now in the Shrine of Fatima Library. It had belonged to Fr. António Reis, of Boleiros, Fatima, and was printed in Lisbon, Officina de Miguel Manescal da Costa, 1762.*

[9] *Cf. Documentação Crítica de Fátima - 1 – Interrogatório aos videntes – 1917 (DCF-1), Fatima, Santuário de Fátima, 1992, doc. 11, notes 79 and 80, and In Lucia's own Words, 9th edition, Fátima, 1995, pp. 215 and 216.*

[10] "I learnt, much later, that without my knowledge, (the Superior) returned the book to my mother on one of the occasions on which she visited me, saying that while I remained at the college I would not be allowed to read that book." (Author's Note).

permission, I gave him the *Imitation of Christ* together with the two needles with which my mother had taught me to do crochet when I was little.[11]

My aunt and uncle left their house and all their other property to my grandparents.

When my grandparents died, it was my mother who inherited the house, the kitchen garden and the well. When my parents died, the property passed to me, and so I had the pleasure of giving it all to Our Lady for her Shrine in Fatima.

I know little or nothing about my mother's childhood. I can only remember listening to one conversation that I have never forgotten as it aroused my interest, though at the time I understood almost nothing about what it meant.

We were all together, seated around the hearth eating our supper – it must have been winter because in the summer we used to eat our supper outside, in the yard, or we used to go to the threshing floor where there was fresh breeze. My sister Gloria said that a young man from the Santa Catarina district had asked if he might go out with her but she was already going out with another young man from Casais, and she did not know which of them would be better. My mother replied: "No-one can tell which of them will be better. What you must do is to choose one who is a good Christian, fulfils his duties, and is a worker, honest and respected. Have nothing to do with anyone who wants to make you commit sin. Rather, turn your back on him as this is a sign that he is neither honest nor chaste, and such people will never make you happy. It is better to remain unmarried than to marry the wrong person."

My father then added: "I am going to tell you something that perhaps I have never yet told you. When I asked your mother to go out with me, the first thing we agreed between us was to keep the flower of our chastity pure until the day of our wedding so that we could offer it to God in exchange for his blessing and any   children He chose to give us. And He has blessed us with this little brood." – With that he made a sweeping gesture towards the growing crops. Only later did I come to understand how, even in the loveliest gardens the poisonous caterpillar appears, nibbling at the loveliest

[11]   *Cf. Fifth Memoir, Appendix, pp 38-39*

flowers and leaving its poisonous trail behind it. But I also came to understand the great and immense mercy of God who, making allowance for human frailty, pardoned the holy King David, when he repented of his sin; the good thief, too, repentant and dying in agony on the cross. Saint Mary Magdalen, repentant and in tears begging for forgiveness; the woman taken in adultery, in front of all her accusers who were ready to stone her. Instead of the final word of condemnation she was expecting to hear from the Supreme Judge, she hears a word of forgiveness, consolation and hope. «Woman, has no-one condemned you? No-one, Lord. Neither will I condemn you. Go in peace and sin no more.»

On one condition: when we sin, we must repent, ask for forgiveness and do penance. If we fall, we must get up again, shake the dust from our clothes and carry on walking more cautiously and taking greater care not to fall again because, though we got up the first time, the second fall could be mortal.

My mother was 21 years of age when she married António dos Santos, a native of Aljustrel, sub-district of Fatima, in Fatima parish church on 19th November 1890.

They settled in her family home so that she could look after her parents who were already quite elderly and ill. Her mother died on 26th November, 1891, just over a year after her marriage, and her father died on 1st August 1907 at the age of 84, exactly five months and 26 days after I was born, so my grandfather surely nursed me in his arms.

Thus, my mother nursed devotedly both her parents and her uncle and aunt, Manuel Maria Ferreira and Maria Isabel Ferreira. All four died in Aljustrel, in their own home, cared for by my mother with the greatest dedication and affection, and were given all the help that was available at that time to alleviate their sufferings.

My mother used to say that after she was married she was greatly helped by my father who did not want her to strain herself unduly in lifting the sick, when necessary, for them to eat and so on. Hence, when he could, he used not to go out to his work in the fields. When he simply had to go, he used to pay a woman to come to our house for the day to help my mother. He was always ready to help in any way that was needed, going to call the doctor when necessary, going to Vila Nova de Ourém to buy the medicines prescribed by the doctor, and going to Fatima to summon the parish priest to administer the Sacraments to those who were sick, etc. At night, when the sick person needed help, he used to send my mother to rest and would himself stay with the person, stretching out on a blanket laid on the floor close to the bed, so as to be there to give the patient whatever they might need.

When my mother's father became more seriously ill, her two oldest daughters were already old enough to help her to look after him. Maria must at that time have been about 15 or 16 and Teresa 13 or 14 or thereabouts. In this way, my mother was preparing them to help, and to take her place in the practice of charity and the care of the sick when she herself might not be able to. And thanks be to God they faithfully followed her example.

My sister Teresa used to describe with a certain pride how, by practising charity, she had managed to save a child's life. It must have been in Alveijar, where she went to live when she married for the second time.

One day they asked her to go and help at a difficult birth. As she did not know what to do, she sent for the doctor. When the child was born, the doctor said to my sister: "Bury this as there's no life in it and it can't survive." But my sister didn't agree with this verdict. When the doctor had gone, she began to attend to the child. She placed the child's mouth on her own and began to breathe into it and warm it. Little by little, it began to move its arms and legs, so she wrapped it in warm blankets and placed it in the bed close to its mother to keep it warm. They tried putting a few drops of milk into its mouth, which the child took and swallowed. Some time later, they managed to make it suck from the mother's breast and in this way it grew strong with no more problems.

When this child was older, my sister took it to her own home on a day when she knew that the doctor was coming, and she asked him to examine it to see if it was in good health. The doctor examined the child and said he found nothing particular wrong with it, that it was a healthy child, normal and well-developed like any other child of its age. Then my sister asked him if he knew who the child was. The doctor said he didn't. Then my sister told him it was the child that he had told her to bury when it was born, and the doctor was astonished.

This was the fruit of the charity taught in the school where my sister learnt it: to love our neighbour as ourselves, to respect and preserve the gift of life that God has given to us, in ourselves and in others, and that God alone has the right to take us from time to eternity. Hence one of his great commandments: "Thou shalt not kill".

I have already described, in the Fifth Memoir, how, during the influenza epidemic, both my mother and my father exposed themselves to deadly contagion, for the sake of charity. And God rewarded them by not allowing anyone in our house to catch it.

4. Unbounded charity

My mother overstepped all boundaries in her practice of charity. One day, she went to a little piece of land we had at the foot of the hill called the Cabeço, also known as Chousa Velha, to fetch a basket of greens. She took me with her for company, as I was still quite small and did not help in the house in any way.

On the way back, we passed a house from which came the sound of someone scolding in a loud voice. My mother opened the gate, went into the yard and knocked at the door. A man with a very cross look on his face came to open it, still grumbling. My mother said :

"Well, then, Senhor Guilherme, what's all this? Is there anything you need?"

The man replied that his house was in a mess, his wife was confined to bed, the baby had been neither washed nor dressed nor fed, and the animals in the pens were crying with hunger, and so on. My mother replied that it was clear that the man's wife had had a baby the evening before, and that she obviously couldn't attend to all those tasks so soon. She added that she would go back home to tell one of her daughters to do her own work, and also kill a chicken to make some broth for the man's wife, who might well still be without food. Then she would come back to look after the man's children and the animals, bath the baby and look after its mother; she also invited the man to come and eat in our house until his wife was fit to see to things once more. The children were to come too and she would look after them until their mother was well again.

The man gratefully accepted her suggestion.

My mother then returned to our house and told my sister Maria what she was to do, adding that she was going back with Teresa, so that she could feed the little ones, wash and dress them, while Mother herself bathed the baby and saw to the mother's needs.

Meantime, the man came running with one of their hens for my mother to kill and make broth for his wife. However, as my sister Maria had already killed one of our own hens, she used the other to replace it.

My mother and my sister Teresa then went back with the man to his house to take care of things and he, already in a good mood, said that he would attend to the animals

When my father arrived home about noon, my mother told him what had happened and asked him to go and call the man in case he felt shy to come and eat with us. So my father went with my sister Teresa, who was taking a pan of broth for the woman to eat. All three came back talking happily. My mother prepared a snack for the man to eat during the afternoon and told him to come back for supper.

When we were all having supper that night, my mother suggested to him that if he would like to spend the next few nights in our house, sharing my brother's room, she would send one of the girls to sleep in his house to keep his wife company, put the children to bed, and keep an eye on them during the night. Then, in the morning, she could tidy the house, get the children up, wash and dress them and then bring them to our house where she would look after them. The man agreed, so my sister Teresa went to spend several nights in that house, I don't remember exactly how many.

Over the next few days, when the man came for his meals, he used to bring a huge basket of greens from his own fields, eggs from his hens, sausages and so on for my mother to use in preparing the next day's snack.

This family was so grateful that the woman used to say that my mother was a second mother to her.

What a good thing it is that in the bad moments in life, God sends us an angel to help us to overcome temptations, to fly from danger and solve our problems!

5 – Children, grandchildren and great-grandchildren

God blessed my parents with seven children :

MARIA DOS ANJOS – She used to work at home as a weaver. She married António dos Santos (Valinho), a native of Currais, in Fatima parish church, on 23rd August 1916. They settled in Aljustrel in a house they themselves built, opposite to our own, on land owned by my parents where they had, by the roadside, a large shed in which they kept the agricultural tools, animal feed and dry wood for the winter. This shed was demolished to make way for the new house.

God blessed my sister's marriage and gave them 8 children:

Teresa who died as a child, having been drowned in a little well in the courtyard outside my parent's house, almost in front of the door into the bakehouse, a little to the left in the Arneiro direction. Beside it there was a big plum tree with a vine growing up through it which used to give lovely bunches of dessert grapes. Through an oversight, the well cover had been left slightly raised and the little one, who used to play there, fell in. When it was realised what had happened, she was already dead. My mother was so upset that she had the well blocked up.

Gloria, who was sent to the Andaluz school in Santarém where she became seriously ill, with typhoid fever, I think, so she returned to Aljustrel with no hope of a cure. She was looked after in her grandmother (my mother)'s house where she died. It was said that she had been a very good girl, quite out of the ordinary in her piety, modesty, purity, seriousness and good reputation. She asked her friends to carry her body to the church and to the cemetery themselves, as a sign that she had kept intact her virginal purity, which she had offered to God out of love. Her companions willingly did what she asked and were deeply grieved by her death.

Maria dos Anjos— Was married in the parish church in Fatima. She established her Christian home in what had been her parents house in Aljustrel. As her mother, my sister Maria, was by then already a widow, she allowed her daughter to live in her house, while she herself moved in with my Mother, to help her, look after her and take care of her in the last years of her life. God blessed

Maria dos Anjos (junior) with 10 children, all of whom were healthy and whom she brought up and educated as good Christians.

Manuel dos Santos Valinho – Married Maria do Nascimento in Fatima parish church. He established his Christian home in Aljustrel where God gave him 10 children, whom he brought up and educated as good Christians. He died after having lived, paralysed, in a wheel chair for 16 years with great resignation during which time he was looked after devotedly and lovingly by his wife and children, who missed him sorely. In imitation of the example of my own parents, who were her grandparents, one of my brother Manuel's daughters, Jacinta, together with a sister-in-law, Lurdes, went to meet a ship that had arrived in Lisbon carrying refugees from Yugoslavia. Though they weren't rich and barely made a living from their work, they went to look for two families:a lady with three children, and another with two. These they brought back home with them. Jacinta took in the lady with the three children and Lurdes the one with two. They took it upon themselves to give them all accommodation, feed and clothe them, and help them in every way for as long as necessary. When a friend of theirs offered them money to help them meet the cost of caring for these families, they refused to accept it saying that they didn't want it to be thought, or said, that they had gone to look for those families out of self-interest, to make money out of them; adding that if she liked, the friend could give the money to the ladies themselves for them to buy something they wanted for themselves that they might not have liked to ask for.

Romana dos Santos Valinho – She helped in the house until she married José de Oliveira in the parish church in Fatima. They established their Christian home in Aljustrel where they built a house. God gave them three children whom they brought up and educated as good Christians.

José dos Santos Valinho – He became a priest, studying and making profession as a Salesian Father. He studied theology in Madrid, Spain, and philosophy in the Salesian University in Turin, Italy. He later taught philosophy in the Salesian Colleges in Estoril and Manique. Later, in Rome, he did a course in spirituality to prepare himself for the office of Master of Novices, which he held for twelve years. He is now vice provincial and director of the Provincial House in Lisbon.

Maria Rosa dos Santos Valinho – Helped with the housework and did dressmaking, having done a dressmaking course at the Sardão College in Vila Nova de Gaia. She married José Reis de Oliveira in Fatima parish church. He, however, emigrated to Australia leaving her with two children and still living with her mother, whom she helped and took care of with the greatest love and dedication until she died. The two children studied in the College run by the Dominican Sisters in Ramalhão. The girl specialised in Germanic studies and now teaches in a grammar school (*liceu*) in Coimbra. After leaving school, her brother got a job as a technician with the T.L.P. Company in Lisbon, where he still works.

Maria Lúcia – Studied in Porto, then took a course in geographical sciences in the University of Coimbra, and now teaches in a grammar school (*liceu*) in Porto. She married a colleague, Carlos Araújo Matos. They settled in Porto and, God has blessed their Christian home with three children.

TERESA DE JESUS ROSA DOS SANTOS – She worked as a dressmaker at home. She married José Pereira in Fatima parish church. They settled in Lomba, where her husband came from and where he already had a house. God gave them 6 children:

Manuel, who joined the Jesuits and became a priest. He worked as a missionary in Mozambique for many years. At the time of the revolution, he was taken prisoner for administering the sacraments of Baptism and Matrimony. After spending some time in prison, he was expelled and returned to Portugal. Later he went to continue his missionary work in France, where he worked with emigrants and where he still is.

The Cardinal of Paris, who visited us here in Carmel, spoke very well of him. The Cardinal told me that he was very pleased with my nephew's apostolate, adding that the church where he works with two other Jesuits is the largest, and most alive, in his diocese, with the largest congregations and the greatest number of people receiving the Sacraments; the people there always find someone ready and willing to receive them.

Maria Amélia – She was educated by the Dorothean Sisters, and made profession as a Dorothean. Feeling called, later, to a life of greater recollection, silence and prayer, she was authorised by the Holy See to transfer to the Carmel in Coimbra, where she made

Solemn Profession. Later she was transferred to the new Carmel which was founded in Braga, where she held the offices of Councillor, Mistress of Novices and Prioress. She is still there.

Julia, who died in infancy.

Etelvina – She went to school with the Dorothean Sisters, and then married João de Sousa Ribeiro. They lived together as good Christians (until) he died of cancer in Lisbon, leaving two children, both of whom are now grown up and have completed their university education.

Maria Carolina – She, too, was educated by the Dorothean Sisters and then did a course for social workers. She married Joaquim de Sousa Ribeiro and settled with him in Porto where he worked as a Council engineer. He died of a coronary (myocardial infarct) leaving 3 children: the oldest has now finished his training as an engineer; the younger two are still studying. Their mother continues to practise as a social worker in the maternity hospital in Porto.

Maria do Rosário – Did her studies in a college in Porto. She married in Fatima parish church. She and her husband settled in Alveijar, where he had been born. A few years later, he emigrated to Venezuela, leaving behind three young children. She got a job in Lisbon looking after children in the *Misericórdia*. The oldest son, Vasco, joined the Navy, where he trained as an engineer: Maria da Piedade studied Fine Arts; José decided to go to Venezuela to work with his father, and is still there.

MANUEL ROSA DOS SANTOS — He worked on the land with his father. He married a girl called Emília, a native of Ramila. He built the first house in Cova da Iria, and there they established their Christian home, having been married in Fatima parish church. A few years later, he emigrated to Brazil, taking his wife and two small children with him. In Brazil, God blessed them with 9 more children. He brought them all up well and gave them a Christian education. When he died, they had all been blessed by God with the sacrament of matrimony and were bringing up their own Christian families.

GLORIA DE JESUS ROSA DOS SANTOS — She did domestic work. She married Francisco Vieira in the parish church in Fatima. They built a house in Cova da Iria where they established their

Christian home. God blessed their marriage with 5 children: one died in infancy; the other four are still alive:

Noé Francisco Vieira – He studied in Lisbon, and got a job in civil aviation, where he is still working.

Preciosa de Jesus Vieira – She married Domingos Carvalhais in Fatima parish church. They emigrated to Brazil where God gave them 3 children: two girls, who have now qualified in medicine. Both of them married doctors and all are working in hospitals in São Paulo. The boy, Augusto Vieira Carvalhais, studied law and is practising as a lawyer in São Paulo. He married in Church and has established a good Christian family.

Maria Rosa dos Santos Vieira – She helped her mother with the domestic work at home. At the request of the Bishop of Assisi, she went to Brazil to help his mother in the organisation and management of a retreat house, while at the same time acting as companion to, and looking after, the lady herself, who was already very old. This lady treated her like a daughter, entrusting everything to her unreservedly, and my niece looked upon her as a second mother. When my sister became ill, Maria Rosa returned from Brazil in order to be with her mother and look after her until the end of her life. After her mother's death, she returned to Brazil and looked after the Bishop's mother until she, too, died. She then married a lawyer, Spencer Campos, in a church in São Paulo and settled in Porto Ferreira, São Paulo, where she still lives, thanks be to God.

José Maria Vieira – He broke off his studies in order to remain at home and help his parents in business. He married Cacilda de Jesus Dias Ferreira in Fatima parish church.[12] God blessed their union with three children: Francisco who studied history at the University of Coimbra; Filomena, who studied Modern Languages and Literature at the same University, and Luís, who interrupted his studies in order to help his father in the business.

CAROLINA DE JESUS ROSA DOS SANTOS – She helped with the housework at home as well as helping her father in the fields; she also learnt to weave, do dressmaking and crochet, and helped our mother to make warm clothes for the winter from the

---

[12] *They were married on 1st April, 1956, in the Chapel of the Apparitions at Cova da Iria.*

wool from our own sheep. She married Manuel Pereira Carvalho in Fatima parish church. They settled and brought up their Christian family in a house belonging to her husband in Casa Velha. God blessed their union with 6 children:

One died in infancy.[13]

Tomé went to be a priest with the Fathers of the Heart of Mary, with whom he studied, made profession and was ordained. Later, he went as a missionary to São Tomé e Príncipe, where he still is. There, with other members of his Congregation, he has built churches, schools and charitable institutes. He is now Vicar General of the Diocese.

Laurentina, whose religious name is Sr. Maria de Belém, went to a school run by the Sisters of the Heart of Mary. She made profession in the Congregation and went as a missionary to Mozambique, where she worked for a number of years. When the country became independent, she returned to Portugal and is now teaching in the Sisters' college in Fatima. She spends any free time she has with her mother, helping her and looking after her, as she is already very old and in poor health and lives alone since the death of her husband. [14]

Francisco emigrated to Germany, where he got a job, married in Church and settled with his wife and one daughter. He is still there.

Manuel did some studies and then got a driving licence, but was killed in an accident while driving an ambulance from Fatima to Coimbra.

José dos Santos also did some studies and then got an office job in Fatima. He married Lúcia Marto in the parish church in Fatima. God blessed their marriage with 6 children whom he brought up and educated as good Christians.

MARIA ROSA, who died at birth.[15]

LÚCIA DE JESUS ROSA SANTOS, the author of this humble memoir who here records the names of her parent's immediate descendants with deep gratitude to God, from whom all gifts and graces come.

---

[13] *Lucia de Jesus dos Santos Pereira died in August 1937.*
[14] *Carolina de Jesus Rosa dos Santos died on 31st March, 1992.*
[15] *Cf. Fifth Memoir, note 14*

6. Faithful to her promises

As a wife, my mother was utterly faithful to her matrimonial vows. Whenever she was called out to go and look after someone who was sick, before leaving the house, she would ask one of the girls to do her work for her and to tell my father, when he came in, where she had gone or where she would be. If it was nearby, my father used to take me by the hand and go, with me, to see whether Mother would be coming home for supper. If the answer was 'yes', then, even if we had to wait for a bit, my father used to wait for her and we would all three come home together to have supper with the rest of the family. But if Mother said she could not leave the sick person, then Father would return home with me, and my sister Maria would stand in for Mother and dish out the supper to each of us.

If my brother or one of my sisters asked Mother for permission to go somewhere unusual, such as a wedding to which they had been invited, a party or a local *festa* and such like, my mother would want to know whether they had already asked my father if they could go. If they said 'no', she would say: "Go and ask him and we'll see what he says". If they went to ask my father first, they would get the same reply: "Go and ask you mother, and we'll see what she says". Thus, they always agreed tranquilly with each other.

If someone came during the night to summon my mother to go and look after someone who was sick, it was my father who got up to see who was at the door. Then he would go to Mother with the message and while she was getting ready, my father would beat the yolks of two eggs in a bowl with a spoonful of honey and brandy for my mother to take before she went out. He would then light the lantern for her to take, to avoid tripping and falling on the way. If it was raining, or cold, he used to wrap her cloak round her, pull her hood over her head, and open the umbrella for her so that she would not get wet or catch cold.

Sometimes, my mother used to describe laughingly these little attentions that my father paid her, and he would reply: "the point is that if you get sick or die, I have no other mother to look after our children."

Thus, being absolutely sure of her fidelity, honour and honesty, my father allowed her to go everywhere without the least worry or suspicion, convinced that she was going to sacrifice herself, for the sake of charity, in order to help and assist whichever neighbour had turned to her for help.

As mother and teacher, she took every care to ensure that her children lacked nothing, within the possibilities open to her at that time. She wanted them to lack nothing that was necessary in the way of food, clothing or warm outer wraps against the cold in the winter.

7. Food

As regards food, my mother made sure that there was enough nourishing food, according to the produce from the land and from the animals, in the various seasons of the year.

Normally, we had a flock of from 25 to 30 sheep, but usually 30. They were large, white, merino sheep which produced plenty of wool, milk and young [nearly all of them bore twin lambs each year] with the result that in the spring the flock almost trebled in number. When this happened, my father used to kill the male lambs to feed the family, whereas the females were allowed to grow, and the best of them were selected to replace the older ewes, which were then sold with the remainder of the female lambs that were not needed, so that the flock returned once more to 30 animals.

My mother and one of my sisters used to get up early to do the milking, in time to leave it to curdle so that each of us could take a large bowl of curds and broken pieces of bread before leaving the house for work. Whatever was left over was used to make cheese.

[In the village] there were two families each of which had a large flock of goats. My mother used to give each of them 6 litres of sheep's milk in exchange for 12 litres of goat's milk – the families were glad to have the sheep's milk to mix with that of the goats, and my mother was glad to have the goat's milk which was better for drinking during the day. She used to put the cans containing the goats' milk into the well, just above the water, hanging on ropes, so that it would keep fresh.

When my father and my brother and sisters returned from the fields in the middle of the morning to spend the hottest part of the day and siesta time in the house, they used to go to the well to get one of these cans and, instead of drinking water, each of them would drink a cup of goat's milk. They did the same in the afternoon before going back out to the fields, once the heat had begun to abate. The same happened with the yield from the evening milking, which was done after the flocks returned from pasture. At supper, after a cooked dish of some kind, we would take another bowlful of curdled milk and bread and, before going to bed, at the end of the evening, we would drink a cup of fresh milk. We also used to give some of the milk to the children who came to our house, and to the young girls who came to learn to weave and to sew, and sometimes also to sick people who had none of their own...

In this way, my mother was a kind of second mother to everyone and many people used to say just this: that they had found in her a second mother and that they turned to her as if she really were their mother.

8. Motherly care

It was in this spirit of motherly goodness that she generously accepted all the children that God sent her. She sacrificed herself for all of them in bringing them up, educating them and helping them to get settled in life to the best of her ability, and not only her own children, but sometimes other people's children too.

She helped to bring up a little girl who was her niece and goddaughter, whose mother had died shortly after she was born. Together with me, she brought up another little orphan girl who had been left without a mother at birth, and she helped to bring up a number of others when their mothers brought them to her to be looked after when they themselves had to go somewhere, or else were unable to look after them. When they asked if they could leave them in our house, my mother always said 'yes, bring them here, they can stay here with Lucia. She will tell them stories, teach them to sing and to dance and they will pass the day quite happily. Off you go and don't worry.' This was her great charity and love for her neighbour for whom she sacrificed herself. But her Lucia was not as yet old enough to attend to all their needs.

If they were very small, she used to rock them in their cradles and sing to make them go to sleep, but if the baby started to cry, my mother, or one of my sisters who was helping with the housework, had to attend to it, give it milk, change it, and so on, which meant a considerable loss of time from the point of view of their work, but that didn't matter to my mother. What mattered was to do good, to help others so that God would help us. It was her great faith and spirit of great confidence in God. And she did it all for charity, accepting payment from no-one.

If the children's parents had still not collected them when it was time for us to eat, they would be given their meal with the rest of us, eating what everybody else was eating.

9. In defence of life

My mother used to say that matrimony was the tree of life that God planted in the garden of the world, and that the fruit of these trees were the children, who had to be brought up with great love and educated with great care because they had come to bring on earth the new life with which God enriches us, and it is they who, in turn, will take care of their parents, in sickness and old age, until God chooses to transfer them from earth to Heaven.

She also used to say that God had forbidden Adam to eat the fruit of the tree because that fruit was the life that belongs to God alone, and that it is for God alone to transplant it from time to eternity, hence his commandment: "Thou shalt not kill".

It was an admirable piece of reasoning implying respect for the gift of life which God alone may transfer from earth to heaven, and God grant that, in spite of our many failings, we may all be granted the grace of being taken from earth to heaven in our Father's arms.

10. More about food

As a mother, she used to enjoy preparing the meals for all the family, and she would vary the menu according to what was available in each season of the year.

We have already seen that breakfast consisted of a large bowl of curds with bread broken up in it. In the middle of the morning, a cup of goat's milk with which anyone who wished could take bread, cheese or olives, which were always available in the drawer of the table in the kitchen, for anyone to take, or to give away if a poor person came seeking alms.

Next came the midday meal, which always consisted of a cooked dish, as at supper. Sometimes the dish would be potatoes stewed together with pork, sausage, cutlets, pig's ears, trotters, etc. At other times the potatoes were stewed with rabbit, hare, partridges or thrushes when my father managed to catch them in the traps and snares he used to set skilfully when necessary; or else sucking pigs, if the sows had very large litters and could not feed them all. At other times, it would be the lambs that my father used to kill in order to feed the family. Sometimes, too, when the clutches of chickens were very large, once the young cock that was to replace the old one had been chosen, the others were all killed and eaten. But the meat was not always stewed. My mother used always to make bread on Saturday, and she used to get the meat ready in large glazed clay roasting pans with small potatoes, or else with potatoes cut into quarters and peas or broad beans, when they were in season. During Lent, when meat was not eaten, the roasting pans were got ready with potatoes and onions cut into slices, together with sliced hard boiled eggs with salt and oil and other dressings. When she removed the bread from the oven, she would turn up the heat and then put in the roasting pans so that the food she had prepared in them could be roasted. Then she would close the door of the oven and only the next day would she remove the pans when everything else was ready for the meal.

When my father caught a lot of game, or when there were a lot of lambs that needed to be killed so that we could have the milk, my mother used to cook larger quantities and then would invite 'Godmother' Teresa to come with her household to sup with us. * They were always very glad to do so. Godmother always used to bring something to complete the feast: sometimes it would be baskets of '*filhoses*' [a kind of fried pastry, Trans.] or pancakes; at other times it would be a kind of small doughnut in syrup, sweet rice, fruit, and white wine from their cellar. There were no vines on my parents' land, except for a few entwined in the old trees, which yielded lovely bunches of dessert grapes. The wine in our house was all from Godmother Teresa's cellar. It would be brought, a few

---

*   *The reference here, and throughout the Memoir, is to Lucia's great-aunt, her father's aunt, Teresa de Jesus, whose husband, Anastácio Vieira, was Lucia's godfather. Cf. above, Fifth Memoir, p. 10 (Translator's note)*

demijohns at a time, as it was needed, because it was my father who tilled her land and so was entitled to a percentage of her crops. On days like that, we used to eat our supper on the threshing floor where there was a very pleasant breeze. We used to put one of the sides of the ox cart in the middle, resting on trestles, and covered with a coarse white linen cloth that had been woven on our own loom. The food we were to eat was placed on that, and all of us, each with a plate in hand, would sit on the various seats dotted around the place. Sometimes, my mother also invited Aunt Olimpia to come with her household, but not so often, as there were a lot of them, and with them, plus Godmother Teresa's household, there was hardly enough room for everyone.

11. Lucia gets up to mischief

That reminds me to record here something that I did, as it shows my mother's great spirit of generosity, always calm and unperturbed.

It was the Feast of All Saints, which at that time was a Holiday of Obligation. The night before, I saw Mother making a cake so that she would have something to give to the children who, next day, would be going from door to door asking: 'Have you a piece of cake for us, Auntie?'

I also saw how, after she had baked the bread and the cake, my mother had put the big roasting pans into the oven with all the food ready for us to eat the next day.

Next day, we all went to the midday Mass as usual. On the way home, while the grownups were walking very slowly and talking, I ran on ahead with a group of children, as I wanted to be the one to give them their cake. But when we got to the house, the door was closed. Then I thought of going to the oven and taking out one of the big roasting pans, which I managed to do with the help of two boys who were bigger than I was. We put it down in the yard on two trestles and with the other children all round me and a big oven fork that my mother kept hanging on the door of the oven in my hand, I started picking out and giving a piece of meat to each one (Mother had already cut the meat before putting it into the pans, so that each person could serve him or herself with one or more pieces without having to cut it) and one or two potatoes. They all ate with gusto, though they were blowing on their hands and shaking them because of the heat. In the meantime, my parents and older brother and sisters arrived, together with all the people who were on their way home to the more outlying parts of Aljustrel, Casa Velha, Eira de Pedra and so on. When they came to the front of our house, they linked up with the group of children who were happily enjoying themselves, eating and laughing without a care in the world. Everyone came in to join us. My sister Maria came up to me and asked me what I was up to. I replied that I had been going to give cake to the children, but that the house door was shut so I was giving them this instead. Whereupon my mother said:

"That's all very well, but now you'll have to give a piece of meat and a potato to all these people too so that they can have a taste."

So I went on using the tip of the fork to fish out little bits of meat or potato, that was already half disintegrated in the bottom of the pan. However, everyone got a little and they went off happy with their children, though it will have taken them some time to clean the children's faces, which were covered with grease that had also dribbled down onto their clothes, but perhaps not quite as much as the oil that flowed down from Aaron's beard on the collar of his robe!

As she left, one of the women thanked my mother and said: "The trouble is that you now have nothing to give to your own family".

"Not at all," my mother replied, "there'll be plenty for everyone."

Then my father reminded us that Mother had invited Godmother Teresa and all her household to come and dine with us. Mother insisted that even so there would be enough as there were three more roasting pans in the oven: one was for our main meal, and the other two were for our supper. Moreover, Godmother Teresa always brought something extra, so there would be plenty, in addition to which we would be roasting chestnuts in the yard that afternoon. We would be spending the afternoon eating chestnuts, and that night no-one would be hungry. And so it turned out. We had a chestnut roasting party in which Aunt Olimpia and all her family, plus the boys and girls who usually came to our yard on Sunday and Holiday afternoons, as well as the men who used to come and play cards with my father, also shared. Everybody took part and there was plenty for everyone. It may well have been Aunt Olimpia who brought the chestnuts and the unfermented wine.

When the Angelus bell rang, my father recited it aloud and all present joined in. The party then broke up and everybody went away very happily and saying 'thank you' for the pleasant afternoon they had had.

After that, we all sat down to supper with Godmother Teresa and her household on the threshing floor. There was plenty for everyone, and some left over. Whenever, afterwards, my mother happened to be speaking about this incident, she used to say: "There was plenty for everyone and some left over; not exactly the twelve baskets from the loaves that Christ multiplied in the desert, but enough to be able to say that there was something left over." That's what Mother was like, always in good humour, always calm and serene. She liked to have these family reunions from time to time. She used to say that they promoted joy, unity and peace between all.

My mother usually prepared a cooked dish for the midday meal. Often it would consist of greens cooked with potatoes and pork, which provided the seasoning and was also a dish in itself. When everything was well done, she would serve up the potatoes, greens and meat. The stock that remained was then thickened with bread that had been crisped and cut into small pieces; this was, in fact, the bread left over from the most recent baking that had gone hard. It was a soup which we all thoroughly enjoyed.

At other times it would be chick-pea soup with greens cooked together with a pork bone to provide the seasoning, and a plate of potatoes stewed with game, when there was any.

Yet again, the meal would consist of chick-peas stewed with meat, and bean soup and greens with a lettuce salad, if there was any.

My mother also used to make omelettes with the eggs from our hens, together with sliced potatoes that had been cooked in their skins. Once the skin had been removed and they had been sliced up, she used to put them in a saucepan with the beaten eggs, slices of sausage and minced lean meat, etc.

When peas and broad beans were in season, these too were stewed with potatoes, sausage, pig's ears etc.; or again, the peas and beans would be made into soup, etc.

In the summer, she used to prepare cold salads with potatoes cooked and sliced, hard boiled eggs, also sliced, tomato, lettuce and green beans, dressed with oil and vinegar in big glazed earthenware salad bowls. Our suppers were more or less the same, as there was not a great deal of variety.

In the months when there was no milk for breakfast, Mother used to make a kind of porridge with maize flour. This she would pour into the plates, making a hole in the middle which we filled with honey and then ate, dipping each forkful in the honey and then putting it into our mouths. At other times, it was grilled sardines, seasoned with oil and vinegar and placed on top of the plateful of porridge or, instead of sardines, mackerel or pieces of cod, grilled and seasoned in the same way.

Sometimes, instead of porridge, we had soaked bread crumbs with pieces of cod, garlic, oil, and eggs which were beaten and added when the dish was almost cooked.

Between meals, there were always olives and cheese in the drawer of the table in the kitchen which anyone could eat when they felt like it. On bread-making days, my mother used to make small rolls for the afternoon snack. These were filled with sausage, grilled sardines or pieces of cod dipped in oil, which kept the bread fresh and made it more tasty.

My mother also used to prepare a bowl for each of us to take at night before going to bed when the evening's work was done. It contained an egg yolk beaten up with a spoonful of honey and a spoonful of brandy. She used to say that it was nourishing, and helped us to relax and sleep well. I think she must have been right as I used to sleep right through the night without waking, and when they called me in the morning, I used to turn over on the other side saying it was early yet.

What I have just described about the food for the time of the year when there was no milk also applies, to some extent, to what we ate during Lent, when we didn't eat meat, and it was nearly always the case that there was no milk during Lent.

As regards fast and abstinence, Mother was very careful to abide scrupulously by the rules. Throughout the whole of Lent we ate no meat, only root crops and fish, cod, mackerel, sardines and shellfish, when there was any. Someone used to go and meet the lorries bringing the fish from the coast at Nazaré to Vila Nova de

Ourém and Torres Novas. They used to stop briefly in front of the church and anyone who wished could go there to buy. We also didn't eat milk or eggs, but I don't remember on which days.

As soon as I was seven, my mother made me keep the full fast and abstinence three days a week, Wednesdays, Fridays and Saturdays. So that I wouldn't be tempted to go to the drawer in the kitchen table to find something to eat, she used to take all the food out and keep it in the barn. Sometimes, my father used to say that I wasn't obliged to fast as I was still very young. But my mother used to say in reply that it was to get me used to it because, she said, you can only bend a cucumber when it's young. When it's fully grown, it will split rather than bend.

I imagine that my mother did the same with all my sisters. I've no idea what happened in other families.

On Holy Saturday, all the big glazed earthenware roasting pans were put into the oven with the Easter lamb — one or more depending on the number of people Mother intended to invite to come and eat with us on Easter Sunday. I think it was one of the days on which she used to invite Godmother Teresa and Aunt Olimpia and their families to come and eat with all of us.

12. The Paschal Visit

During Holy Week, my sisters' work was to whitewash the whole house, inside and outside, to clean and polish, in order that everything would be in perfect readiness for the reception, on Easter Sunday, of the Risen Lord in the person of the Parish Priest who would come to wish us a happy Easter in the Lord's Name.

When the Parish Priest was getting near, and while he was visiting the people next door, my father used to set off three fireworks in our yard in honour of the Resurrection of Jesus Christ. Then he would run indoors so as to be kneeling with all the family in the front room ready to receive the Paschal Visit, kiss the crucifix, and receive the blessing which the parish priest gave in the name of the Risen Lord Jesus. Then I, being the youngest, was the one deputed to present the Easter gift to the parish priest. This consisted of a lamb which would have been chosen from among the best of the flock [as it was] the Paschal Lamb, decorated with a big bow made with silk ribbon round its neck, with its front and hind legs bound, and placed in a wicker basket with flowers. One of the men who accompanied the parish priest would take it from me and put it in a cart that was coming behind. Then the parish priest would tell me to put my hand into a bag of sugared almonds carried by another man, and take out as many as I wanted. But my hand was very small, so I could only take out a few. Because of this, the parish priest used to tell me to put my hand in as many times as necessary to fill the two pockets in my dress (up to the age of six, girls wore dresses; only after they were six did they begin to wear a blouse and a skirt, which explains why in the photographs Jacinta is sometimes seen wearing a dress and in others a blouse and skirt). Then the parish priest would place several handfuls of almonds for all the family on the table in the outer room, and then depart after giving us his blessing.

13. Fruit trees

My parents also had enough fruit to last throughout the year, with what my mother stored in the attic, spread out on the floor and hung from the roof beams.

In the courtyard of the house there were five huge fig trees: one of these was opposite and a little bit away from the kitchen door. Its branches used to trail across the roof of the sheepfold and over the entrance to the shed for the oxen. The other four were on the far side of a small well which used to be just beyond the entrance to the bakehouse, two on each side of the path that led to the well. The tips of the branches of the two on the right-hand side hung down over the threshing floor, while the tips of the left-hand branches were interlaced, over the pathway, with those of the two fig trees to the left of the path leading to the well. My father used to prune them in such a way that, when we went to the well, it was like walking through a tunnel.

Just above a small supporting wall, on the far side of our bake-house, which separated our yard from Godmother Teresa's property, we also had a small piece of ground where there were plum trees and two more fig trees.

To get to the well, one had to go down a flight of stone steps from the yard. Beyond the steps there were two lemon trees in a corner, and then some more fig trees which my father, later on, gave to a neighbour who complained that he hadn't a single fig tree near the house from which to gather dessert figs. On the other side of the path, to the right as one goes towards the well, there was yet another fig tree which, together with the others I have already mentioned, gave an abundant crop of figs to eat, feed to the animals and to dry to eat throughout the year.

As one approached the well, there were some chestnut trees on the left-hand side. When in season, these yielded plenty of chestnuts for quite a long time. Mother used to keep them spread out on the floor in the attic.

On the right as you approached the well, there were pear and apple trees – I don't remember how many; beside the well there were some "Queen Claudia" plum trees, and these my mother used to dry for us to eat during the year. Behind the plum trees there were some olive trees. A little way below the well, on the left, there were two big old apple trees with four vines wound around the trunk which yielded lovely bunches of dessert grapes. The trees yielded very few apples, but my father said that he did not dig them up and put others in their place because though they yielded no apples, the grapes were good and were handy for us to eat.

In the Mouriais, there were a further two old apple trees, beyond the cultivated part, each with two vines entwined in its branches, these also yielded a plentiful crop of grapes.

There were two more old pear trees in the Cova da Iria which bore very big pears. They were known as 'winter pears', and they kept for a long time on the tree. These trees, too, had four vines wrapped around the trunk, two in each. The vines yielded lots of bunches of long black hard grapes which my mother kept for a long time hung from the roof rafters, together with lots of others from the grapes that were left over from the time when we ate them while they were in season. She also kept pears and apples there. I was the one who had to go and hang them in the lower part of the roof where neither my mother nor my sisters could reach, and in some places even I could only do so on my knees. Mother also kept the pears and apples spread out on straw on the floor of the attic. The potatoes that were needed from day to day were also kept there. Anything that did not fit was stored, together with other crops for which we had no storage space in the house, in a house that had belonged to our ancestors but which was unoccupied. Godmother's wine vault was on the ground floor. The upper floor was reached by means of a flight of stone steps which gave onto Godmother Teresa's yard. It was here that her crops were stored, together with part of ours [including my father's share in Godmother's crops, as it was he who cultivated her land for her]. When what we had in the house was used up, we used to go there to get what was needed, or what was to be sold together with what Godmother was selling. A number of trays – I don't remember how many – were also kept there. These were used to store the cheese that we used in the months when there was no milk to make fresh cheese.

We have already spoken about the pear and apple trees in our garden. There were two more apple trees on another piece of land, Sesmarias, while in Mouriais and the Cova da Iria the trees were of the pippin variety, bearing long white apples with a hard skin that were very tender and tasty to eat. They remained on the tree until pruning time; we only went to pick them when there were no more of the other varieties that did not keep so well, and we only brought them in, in baskets, as and when they were needed. At pruning time, all the fruit that had remained on the tree was harvested.

Thus, fruit figured largely in our diet.

14. Lucia up to mischief again

Speaking of fruit reminds me to record something that happened when I was small and did not yet know how to offer sacrifices to God. It will show what I was like. I imagine it must have been around Christmas time, which was the time when my mother used to send gifts to certain people. She took three fine bunches of grapes from the attic, arranged them nicely in a little basket (they used to tell me that it was in that basket that I came down from heaven with flowers) and told me to take it to the parish priest in Fatima. I went, but on the way I began to nibble at the bunch which was on top: I picked off a grape here and a grape there, with the result that when I got to the church square, I realised that that bunch was no longer fit to be offered to the parish priest. So I ate the rest of the grapes and threw the empty stalk over a low wall bordering a property next to the cemetery. I then calmly crossed the square in front of the church and went to deliver the two remaining bunches. I climbed the presbytery steps and knocked at the door. It was the parish priest's sister who came to take the grapes from me, smiling and saying 'thank you'.

I went back down the steps and crossed the square to go and make a visit to the Blessed Sacrament in the Church – my mother always urged us, whenever we went to Fatima, never to come away without first going into the church and making a visit to the Blessed Sacrament. As I did so, I remembered that if the parish priest were to say to my mother that there had been only two bunches of grapes and not three, she would scold me and would want to know what I had done with the other one. With this fear in my mind, I went into the church, knelt down near the altar rails and my prayer was: "Please don't let the parish priest tell Mother that there were only two bunches of grapes and not three." I prayed I don't know how many Our Father's and Hail Mary's like that.

On the way home, I kept on repeating the same prayer: "Don't let the parish priest tell Mother that there were two bunches of grapes and not three, Our Father; that there were two bunches and not three, Hail Mary; that there were two bunches and not three, Our Father...."

And God heard my prayer, as I believe my mother never got to know, as she never said anything to me about it.

When I think back on this incident, I think: it is part of human frailty to stumble and fall. It belongs to God to have mercy, grant pardon, and the grace to enable us to pick ourselves up and set out again on the right road.

And so, today, I pray in the lovely canticle [in the book of] Samuel :

«It is the Lord who gives life and death,

He sends men to the grave and back;

it is the Lord who makes poor and makes rich,

who brings down low and raises men on high» (I Sam. 2, 6-7).

I believe what I have just written answers the many questions about the kind of food we ate, while at the same time showing how careful my mother was, in the fulfilment of her duty, as a Christian and as the mother of a family, and how well she was able to harmonise the two things which cannot be separated from one another.

15. Caring for our clothes

I now propose to describe how, as mistress of the house, my mother saw to the clothing for all the family, according to the customs of the time.

Everyone had their own clothes for weekdays. Mother was always careful to see that everyone in the house had a change of clothing ready on the hooks in the bedrooms, to change into when necessary: in the winter if one got wet in the rain, in the summer if one came in perspiring because of the heat.

Summer clothing was light, made of printed cotton, striped calico or other similar materials. In the winter a much thicker material was used. The menfolk wore twill and a thick woollen material the name of which I cannot now remember. Their overcoats were made of thick wool and their underclothes of flannel. My mother used to make their stockings from the wool from our sheep, as well as their vests, as she did for herself and for the girls, who also wore woollen serge skirts woven from sheep's wool on our own loom. These were used to wear in the winter, very full, together with a deep red strip of material, in the form of a cloak, for warmth, which was gathered at the neck with a collar.

When the lambs and the ram were sheared, the yield was approximately 31 fleeces of wool. Mother, with some of my sisters, used to wash them carefully, then they were sent to the carders who turned them into fine bundles – just like raw cotton.

My mother used to pick out what she needed for our clothes and then send it to be spun and dyed various colours. The rest she would sell.

When the wool came from the factory in skeins, it was wound [into balls] and then the various items of warm winter clothing were woven on the loom, while the stockings and other clothes were crocheted. My mother taught me to crochet when I was very small, first narrow bands of lace to decorate one's underclothes; later she taught me to work with wool.

Once I asked my mother to let me make a red woollen jumper for myself. Mother said 'yes', and taught me how to do it. When it was finished, it so happened that a poor girl from Moita, 'Uncle' Lampião's daughter, came to our house begging. My mother picked up the jumper which I had just finished making, and as it fitted the little girl, she gave it to her. I was upset at this and I said to my mother :

"So you gave her the jumper I had made. And now I have nothing new to wear on All Saints' Day."

My mother replied saying that the little girl's clothes were in tatters and that she was cold...[She went on to say] that she would make another for me, which would be better as she would teach me to include some fancy work in it. So I grabbed the crochet needle, and sat down on the floor next to my sister Teresa, who was sewing, with the bag of wool in front of me, and promptly started to make the second jumper. I kept on asking Mother was it time yet to start the fancy work: But my mother kept saying no, not until the end when it is ready, so I kept going until I got to that point. Then my mother taught me to put on a white collar, as well as some white turn-back cuffs, and a belt to tie round it.

On All Saints Day (known as little cake day), I went off to Mass in my red jumper with its white collar and cuffs and white belt, with a blue wool skirt my mother had made for me in crocheted sections as if it were pleated. Everyone said I looked very nice, and I was filled with vanity.

When we came out of the Church at the end of Mass, I met, in the square, the little girl to whom my mother had given the first jumper I had made. I asked her if she liked it, and at the same time showed her the one I was wearing, saying that I had made them both. The grown ups, seeing the two children deep in conversation, drew near to listen and see what it was all about. They asked my mother whether it was true that I had made the two jumpers. Mother said yes, it was. Then they praised me and congratulated me, which flattered my vanity. It was an innocent kind of vanity, derived from ignorance of the deceitful nothings of the world. As yet I did not know what the Imitation of Christ tells us: "Vanity of vanities, all is vanity except to love and serve God".

After that, I asked my mother to let me make a blue woollen shawl with red stripes to wear for the first time at Christmas, when I went to kiss the Child Jesus.* My mother said I could, but that I would have to make two, one for myself and the other to give to one of the little poor girls who went around begging and had none.

*   *Cf. Fifth Memoir, English edition, note ** on p. 24.*

I did not think there would be time, but I got hold of the wool and, sitting down on the ground, started to crochet busily.

When my father returned home that evening, I said to him :

"Now don't come asking me to dance, Papa, because I can't go."

"You can't? What has happened then?" he asked.

I told him that I had asked Mother to let me make a blue shawl with red stripes to wear for the first time when I went to kiss the Child Jesus at Christmas and that Mother had said I could, but that I had to make two, one for myself, and the other to give to one of the poor children who went around begging and had none of their own. I added that I did not think there would be time [to make them both].

My father replied :

"You'll have time all right, I'll help you."

"But you don't know how to crochet!"

"That's true, he replied, "but I can wind the wool for you."

And he drew a chair up close to me. He then went to the drawer of the machine to get an empty cotton spool, took a skein of wool out of the bag, threaded it into the wool winder and sat down beside me to wind it.

My mother, who was busy in the kitchen, realised what was happening and came in smiling and hugged my father from behind saying:

"What a good man you are! But look, you don't wind wool in the same way as cotton. You wind wool on your fingers so as to make a fluffy ball so that the wool does not lose its softness."

And she taught my father how to wind the wool on the fingers of his left hand. My father looked at my mother smiling and said:

"Now I have learnt something else: to wind wool on my fingers."

And with the squeaking sound of the wool winder, the thump of the combs in the loom where my sister Maria was weaving, and noise of the sowing machine wheel which my sister Teresa was turning slowly, he began to sing :

> The name of Mary
> How good it is
> Save my soul
> For it is yours.

For it is yours
It has to be
Save my soul
When I come to die

When I come to die
When my days are over
Take my soul
To a good place

To a good place
To Paradise
Save my soul
On the day of judgement.

Gradually, the voices of my mother, who was busy in the kitchen, of my sisters who were working at the loom and the sewing machine close by, and of his little top, seated on the floor at his feet busy with her crochet needle, were added to those of my father. When he stopped, I asked, thinking of the phrase "take me to paradise":

"Papa, is the paradise to which Our Lady is going to take us the one where Adam ate the apple?"

"No," he replied. "The place Our Lady is going to take us to is Heaven".

"Oh, well, that's alright then," I said. "Because I don't want to go to the one where Adam ate the apple. There are snakes wrapped around the trunks of the trees there, and so you can't eat those apples. But those snakes were able to talk, and the ones you see when you go up on the heath don't."

"No they don't," my father replied. "The fact is that they lied when they deceived Eve so that she would disobey God and eat the apple. So God punished them. They were struck dumb and forced to slide along the earth."

In the meantime, my mother came to call us to supper as everything was ready. Patting me on the shoulder, she said:

"So you see, little one, you must not tell lies, otherwise God will punish you as He punished the snakes and you will be struck dumb like them and made to crawl along the ground and eat dust".

"Oh, but I don't tell lies."

And we went to have our supper.

I don't remember quite what we ate that day, perhaps potatoes cooked with greens and codfish, or grilled sardines, or else cooked with pork meat; and the stock that was left over was used to make a soup with pieces of the bread left over from the last baking toasted and, when available, potatoes stewed together with rabbit or some of the birds that were already pecking at the olives and that my father used to snare very cleverly; or else it would be omelettes made with the eggs from our hens with sliced potatoes, sausage and little pieces of bacon or strips of cod. Sometimes, the soup would be made from bread in sugared wine* or the slices of toasted bread would be filled with meat, dipped in egg and fried, etc., as, coming up to Christmas, the sheep were no longer in milk until their young were born, so we couldn't have the bowls of 'clabber' (curdled milk) at night and in the morning, nor could we have the cups of milk in the middle of the morning and afternoon, for the afternoon snack and at night. But my mother, ever attentive, foresaw everything and made sure that we went short of nothing that we needed. At the same time, she took advantage of every opportunity to urge us always to tell the truth. She said that she herself had always to tell the truth, even if it were against herself, because, she said, anyone who tells the truth does not deserve to be punished, and God is the truth that does not deceive itself and cannot deceive us – that's what was taught in the catechism at that time. Jesus Christ says in the Gospel: «I am the Way, the Truth and the Life; whoever follows me does not walk in darkness but has the light of life». My mother had this engraved in her spirit and she walked in the light of this Life.

It was for this reason that she was so upset at the time of the apparitions, as it seemed to her that such a thing could not be true. "Are we worthy of such a thing? Get this out of your head, child, and tell the truth!"

My mother was right. Humanly speaking, it was impossible. We were very far from being worthy of such a grace! What she did not realise was that, from one moment to the next, God is able, from mere stones, to raise up children to Abraham. God allowed it all to happen as it did so that she could ascend the steps of her steep Calvary by the light of faith alone.

*   *Known as 'tired horse soup'. (Translator's note)*

16. The virtuous woman

Now when I read in Sacred Scripture what the Book of Proverbs has to say about the virtuous woman, I seem to see there a portrait of my mother: «Who can find a virtuous woman? She is far more precious than jewels. The heart of her husband trusts in her, and he will lack nothing (...). She opens her hand to the poor and reaches out her hands to the needy. She is not afraid of snow for her household for they are all clothed in double garments. She makes coverings (....); Strength and beauty are her clothing, and she laughs at the time to come. She opens her mouth with wisdom, and the teaching of kindness is on her tongue. She looks well to the ways of her household, and does not eat the bread of idleness (...). Charm is deceitful, and beauty is vain, but a woman who fears the Lord is to be praised. Give her the fruit of her hands and let her works praise her in the gates of the city» (Prov. 31, 10-11; 20-22; 26-27; 30-31).

«God protects her with his presence. God is close to her and she shall not be moved. Therefore her lamp shall not be put out» (Ps. 45, 6a; Prov. 31, 18).

In his allocution to newly married couples, Pius XII said : "The family has its own radiant sun, the wife. Hear how scripture puts it: "The grace of a diligent wife will charm her husband. A holy and honest woman is an inestimable grace. Like the sun rising over the mountains of the Lord, so is the beauty of a good wife in a well-kept house. Yes; the wife and the mother is the radiant sun of the family. She is this sun by her generosity and forgetfulness of self, by her unfailing readiness, by her watchful and prudent delicacy in all matters which can add joy to the lives of her husband and her children. She spreads around her light and warmth. And if you can say that a marriage augurs well when both partners seek the happiness of the other rather than their own, this noble feeling and intention is more especially the quality of the wife, although it concerns both husband and wife. It is born of the very pulse of her mother's heart and its wisdom; that wisdom which, if it receives bitterness, gives only joy; if it receives belittlement, returns only dignity and respect. It is like the sun which brightens the cloudy morning with its dawning ray and in its setting gilds the evening shower.

The wife is the radiant sun of the family with the brightness of her glance and the ardour of her word. A glance and a word which gently enter the soul, bending it and making it softer and lifting it out of the tumult of passion, and recalling her husband to joy in the good and in familiar conversation, after a long day of uninterrupted and often painful work, whether professional or agricultural, in commerce or in industry. The wife is the radiant sun of the family by her natural candour, by her simple dignity, and by her Christian and decent behaviour. She is the sun of the family as much by her collectedness of mind and uprightness of heart as in the subtle harmony of her bearing and her dress, in her becomingness and in her behaviour at once reserved and affectionate. Little signs of feeling, shades of facial expression, ingenuous silences and smiles, an approving movement of the head give to her the grace of some choice yet simple flower which opens its petals to receive and reflect the colours of the sun. If you could only know what deep feelings of affection and gratitude such an ideal wife and mother arouses and imprints in the hearts of her husband and children!" (Alloc. of Pius XII, 11th March, 1942).

And we also read in the Book of Sirach (26, 13, 15-16) «A wife's charm delights her husband. A modest wife adds charm to charm. Like the sun rising in the heights of the Lord, so the beauty of a good wife is the 'light of her house'».

As I finish writing this, I feel welling up in my heart a hymn of thanksgiving to God our Saviour for the gifts of nature and of grace with which He deigned to endow the one chosen by Him to confer life on me, and to bring me up to fix my eyes on heaven.

She was not rich in the things of this world, nor in the human sciences that people set so much store by, but she was rich in the gifts of nature and of grace, of faith, hope and love, those gifts which most enhance our value, which do not fade, and the fruits of which abide with us in time and in eternity. In the words of the unceasing hymn of eternal praise of the glory of Our God and Saviour:

> All the earth is filled with his praise;
> The heavens proclaim the glory of his love;
> Hosanna to the son of David.
> Blessed is he who comes in the name of the Lord!

17. Christian charity

From what I have already written and from what I propose to write about the few years during which I had the happiness of living with my mother, we shall see how everything seems to spring from the whole of her activity, so naturally, with utter simplicity and humility, just as the little streams that water and fertilise the land bubble forth from a spring of clear water.

Already in the Fifth Memoir, I have described how our house was a kind of open house where all were welcome. The door was opened with the same glad welcome, service and charity to anyone and everyone who came knocking at it.

It seemed as if my mother could only say 'yes'. She never refused her services when asked, and, on many occasions, it was she herself who offered her help.

The various episodes in her life that I have already described, and those that I have yet to recount, reveal her great spirit of sacrifice and charity, always hard-working and ready to help and serve anyone who approached her.

I have also related in the Fifth Memoir how my parents provided not only material help, but, at times, even shelter for the poor who came to them in need.

Among many others, a poor person from somewhere near Minde appeared one day asking for help and shelter. My mother said 'yes'. The woman had a little girl with her who was very dirty and her clothes all torn.

When my mother saw the state the little girl was in, she told my sister Maria to heat some water to give the little one a wash, while she went to see whether she could find some clothes for her among those that I no longer used as I had grown out of them. My sister went and, while she was waiting for the water to heat, she took the little one out to the barn where there was a stone sink in which we used to wash ourselves, using watering cans to make a kind of shower. [Once we had soaped ourselves, we used to pour the water from the spout of the watering can all over ourselves from head to foot.] This sink was raised up a bit from the ground on stones; at the bottom there was a hole with a pipe through which the water flowed into buckets and was then used to water the pots of flowers that my mother kept on the low wall that separated our yard and Godmother Teresa's property, and thence on down to the well. At other times, the water was emptied onto the manure heap to promote decomposition; the heap was on the lower level, in the little courtyard in front of the entrance to the cattle shed.

[My sister's intention was] to undress the little girl and put her in the sink in order to wash her, but as soon as she found herself in the sink the little girl started to howl, and wanted to jump out, so much so that my mother and the child's mother had to go and help to hold her and give her a shower with the spout of the watering can. I was out in the yard playing. From time to time, I came back into the house and went to peep in at the door of the barn, but when I saw three women around that little girl to hold her still, and heard her cries, I ran away and went back outside. In the end, they managed to wash and dress her and comb her hair, tying her plaits with a piece of red ribbon that they used to use for me. It wasn't mine – nothing was mine even then – it belonged to anyone who happened to need it, and so it has always been throughout a long life, and will be to the end, please God: «Do not be over-anxious about what to wear or what to eat, because your Father who is in Heaven knows that you need these things, and will take care of you.» It was along this path that my mother led my footsteps from the earliest days of my life. Even in my cradle I shared my mother's milk with another child, a little orphan girl whose mother had died when she was born, and I did not suffer in consequence, for I grew up strong and healthy, without any kind of illness.

Pope St Leo the Great says: "Let no one fear the failure of his wealth by such payments, for liberality itself is a great fortune, nor can one lack the means to practise that generosity whereby Christ feeds others and is himself fed in them. In all this work his hand intervenes to increase the quantity of bread as it is broken, and multiply it as it is distributed." (Sermon 10 on Lent, cf. The Divine Office, Second Reading for Lent, Tuesday, Week 4).

With these humble thoughts I interrupted what I was saying about the little girl, so now I'll continue [that story].

When they had finished dressing her, my mother called me and told me to take her outside to play with me until they called us for supper. I took her by the hand and took her out to the threshing floor. I sat down with her on the ground and asked her if she knew how to play the stone game, but she said no; whether she knew how to sing and dance, and again she said no; whether she knew how to make the Sign of the Cross, again no; did she know the Our Father and the Hail Mary, no, she didn't; had she ever seen the candles that Our Lady and the Angels light and place at the windows of heaven to light us on our way, but again the answer was 'no'.

"Doesn't your father teach you these things, then?"

"No".

"What does he do?"

Then she said: "My father scolds a lot, he beats us and eats everything that's given to my mother".

In the meantime, my father arrived:

"Hello so you have a nice little companion."

Then he sat down on one of the seats at the edge of the threshing floor. I ran to sit on his knee. I wanted to bring the little girl with me but she, being shy and timid, refused and remained sitting forlornly where she was on the ground. Then my father went over to her with me, fondled her, and with some difficulty we managed to get her to stand up. Then my father sat us both, one on each knee, and I began to tell him that she knew nothing, not even how to make the Sign of the Cross. Then my mother came to call us to supper. So we went. My mother sat her on a little stool next to me, to encourage her to eat, and in this way she gradually lost her shyness and timidity, and began to laugh and to play. She slept with her mother in the weaving room, on a mattress laid on the floor and covered with blankets that my mother kept for just such occasions. The next morning, my mother gave them their breakfast just like ours, and then they were bidding us goodbye, but the little one did not want to go. She clung on to me saying: "I won't go, I don't want to go!" Only when her mother took her by the hand and said that if she stayed they would put her in the sink to wash her again, was she persuaded to go. I stood with my mother on the steps that lead up from the street until they had disappeared around the bend in the road. The little one kept running back to say "goodbye" and wave her hand.

Throughout my life I have often thought about this little girl when thinking of so many others as unhappy or even more unhappy than she was, to whom God did not give the grace of being born into a Christian home, a humble one, but no matter.

What matters is that it should be blessed by God with the gifts of faith, hope and love, where all live together in peace, joy and well-being, understanding one another, forgiving one another and serving one another with a view to the common good, each one sacrificing him- or her- self and all working to ensure that the others lack nothing. And here let me quote what St. Paul wrote in this connection: «He who does not work let him not eat». [II Thess. 2, 10]. And I would add to that: "And let him not drink anything but water, lest he die of thirst."

In our village of Aljustrel and in the nearby villages of Casa Velha and Eira da Pedra, there was no one so poor that they needed to go around begging. If someone was in need, the neighbours would rally round to help them, so that they never lacked the necessities of life.

There was no thieving. Very often, when the mistress of the house went out she felt so secure that she would leave the door open, or the key in a hole in the wall where the neighbours knew where to find it.

The poor people who came begging were from more distant places; this is why they asked for shelter because it was too far to return to their own village.

Another time, another woman came to our house begging. My mother, with my two sisters Maria and Teresa, who were normally at home, had all three gone out, I don't remember where. They may well have gone to Fatima to help the parish priest's sister to sweep, and clean the church and put fresh flowers on the altars. They used to do this on certain days and on those occasions, all three used to go in order to get done quickly. Only I myself and my brother were at home; he was cleaning the cattle sheds and I was playing in the yard.

When I realised that there was a poor beggar woman knocking on the door, I went and called my brother to come and give her an alms. So he came, went into the kitchen, opened the drawer in the kitchen table where my mother had left a pork bone with quite a bit of meat on it intending, when she returned, to use it for the family meal. My brother took the meat. He then lifted down a whole loaf from the tray that hung from the ceiling – where my mother used to put the bread to cool when she took it out of the oven – and went to give the lot to the woman. As he gave it to her, he realised that it would not fit in the bags she was carrying. She began to tuck up her apron, but my brother told her to wait. He then went back into the house and went to the weaving room where he grabbed a bag that was hanging on the beams of the loom in which the balls of thread to fill the shuttles were kept. He tipped them all into a basket, put the meat bone and the bread into the bag and gave the lot to the woman. The woman was astonished and said:

"Are you giving me all of this, or do you want me to bring the bag back the next time I come?"

My brother replied :

"Take the lot and pray for me".

The woman said :

"I will most certainly pray that God will give you health and good luck in life."

And threading the handles of the bag on her arm, she sat the child on top of the handles and set off up the road, I presume praying.

Shortly afterwards, my mother returned with my two sisters. Maria went straight to the loom and then realised that the bag was missing. She called to my mother to know what had happened to it. And I was at once called to account!

"Did you take the bag from here?"

So I explained what had happened and that it had been Manuel who had given it to a poor woman with the meat bone that had been in the drawer, and a loaf. My mother smiled as she listened to my story. But Maria said that she needed the bag as she had not got another one to put the balls of thread in, and that they couldn't be kept in the basket, and so on. My mother replied :

"Don't worry. We can make another bag. We have lots of pieces left over from the dressmaking. Lucia will make one." Then she took the bag of pieces and told me to sit down beside my sister Teresa, so that she could teach me how to cut them straight and all the same size, and then stitch them together. She cut a piece of unbleached cotton for the lining of the bag and said :

"This is the size it has to be."

And there I had to sit, not able to play. I do not remember exactly how many days it took me to make the bag. At night when we were at supper, my mother called on me to tell my father what had happened, and to go and get the patchwork bag to show him how far I had got with making the new one. My father listened smilingly to my story. Then, he looked at the patches which I had already sewn together and said :

"Good! Soon you'll be a dressmaker who can take Teresa's place when she gets married."

This praise pleased me and encouraged me to go on with the work, which was my very first piece of sewing.

When I was still quite small, I used to like to go and sit on the pedals of the loom and seesaw up and down. And although my mother had told me that she did not want me to go there, one day I went when she and Maria were out of the house. Unluckily, one of the cords connecting the pedal to the warp ends broke and the pedal fell to the ground. I was terrified, thinking that my mother when she came would scold me and smack me. Because of this fear, as soon as I heard her coming with Maria I crept under the table in the kitchen. I sat on the floor with my back to the wall of the barn and peeped from under the table to see them when they came. In due course they did come, and when they entered the house, Maria went straight to the loom and immediately realised that the pedal had fallen and the cord had broken. She called to my mother to come and see, saying that Lucia had undoubtedly been swinging on it.

"But where is she?"

And they started to look for me while I, without replying, peeped out from under the table. Eventually, Maria discovered my hiding place and when I saw them coming with hands raised to catch hold of me, I began cry out and beat my heels and my hands on the ground. When they saw me like that, they thought it was funny, so they turned away laughing. Maria went to the loom to mend the cord. My mother sat down beside my sister Teresa in the front room and began to sew. When I saw them like that, I was no longer afraid, so I came out of my hiding place and slowly went and sat on my mother's lap, caressing her and saying :

"You won't smack me, will you?"

My mother replied:

"No, you rascal. When are you going to begin to do what you're told? I've told you lots of times not to go near the loom!"

And I replied:

"I know you did, but the cord broke."

"Yes, it was the cord that broke," my mother replied, "but why did the cord break? Wasn't it because you were disobedient and were see-sawing on it."

"Yes, I was, but it was the cord that broke".

"What a little rascal! You're a true child of Adam!"

"But Papa's name is not Adam!"

"No, it's not!" my mother replied. "Out you go and play".

So I went, but I spent the rest of the day thinking about being a child of Adam. At night, when we were all at supper, I said to my father that Mother had said that I was a child of Adam.

My father replied:

"So am I, and so are we all."

My mother interrupted and said to me:

"Alright then, tell him why I said that you were a child of Adam. Go on, tell your father why I said it. Wasn't it because you were disobedient and were swinging on the pedals of the loom?"

I replied:

"Yes, it was, but it was the cord that broke".

My father laughed and I said to him:

"Papa, I have never even seen Adam!"

"No, of course not", he replied. "He died many years ago".

"Oh! But what did he die of?"

"He died because he did what you do sometimes, when your mother tells you not to eat fruit that is green and you eat it. God said to him not to eat the apple, and he disobeyed and ate it. Then God punished him and he died."

"Oh! Now I understand. The apple was green and upset him, and his mother wasn't there to brew tea for him and he died."

My mother said:

"And that is what will happen to you if you continue to eat green fruit. I won't brew tea for you and you'll die like Adam did."

"Yes, but I will never again eat green fruit, oh no, certainly not."

18. Popular songs

As I describe these little incidents that took place in the heart of a poor humble family, and as 'poor' is the word I have used to describe them, I ask myself: What is the point of all this? And the answer is: I don't know. I am doing it for the love of God, out of obedience, since my superiors have asked me to do it; I am doing it in response to the request of the Rector of the Shrine of Our Lady of Fatima, who asked me not to leave out any detail that I can remember of the life of my family. The day-to-day life of a family is made up of so many tiny details and little incidents that I cannot possibly describe them all. Hence, I am like a butterfly fluttering about and alighting, from time to time, on one or other of the humble flowers of the field. Very often, as a child, I used to run and try to catch one, attracted by the beautifully variegated colours of its wings. In the same way, now, I am picking out here and there the things that it seems to me I can best offer to the Lord as a loving hymn of praise to give Him pleasure and glory on earth and in heaven for always.

Thus I sing and pray in the words of Psalm 70:

«My mouth is filled with your praise,
when I sing to you, my lips shall rejoice
for as long as my song lasts.»

That reminds me to record here the words of one of the songs which I learnt when I was small and which I sing at appropriate moments even now, as they remind me of the presence of God, and His fatherly love, watching always over his children. They also make me hope that His children, too, will think of Him and will know how to return Him love for love:

CHORUS

There is a little window in heaven
You can see Portugal from there (repeat)
When God is feeling sad
He goes and sits near it   (repeat)

1
The bell is the heart of the village
The heart is the people's bell;
One is heard when it rings
The other beats when it feels.

2

Beside this window
God sits to contemplate
Resting on me
The light of his gaze

3

I raise my eyes
Seeing the sky so bright
It was God smiling at me
Listening to me sing

4

If only I had wings
On this lovely day
To fly up to heaven
And be with the Virgin Mary!

19. A lesson for a lifetime

My mother was very gentle and affectionate. She took great care to ensure that nothing that was needed was lacking. However, when it was a question of whims and lack of courtesy, she was very demanding and austere, and would let nothing pass.

One day, she had cooked some broad beans, stewed with potatoes cut into small pieces with slices of sausage, for our mid-day meal. When we had all assembled in the kitchen for the meal, my mother was serving out the food onto each plate, as she always did, beginning with my father and the older members of the family. Being the youngest, I was last, as I usually was. When Mother passed me my plate, I refused to take it, saying that I didn't eat beans as I didn't like them. My mother replied:

"Well, little one, in this house you don't eat only what you like, but what there is to eat, like everyone else; so until you eat your beans, you'll get nothing else.

With that, she put the plate down on the table, expecting me to take it and begin to eat. Everyone told me to eat as it was very good, but my caprice would not let me. From time to time, my father reached out with a bean or a piece of sausage on his fork, which he wanted to put into my mouth to taste it and see that it was good. But no! Nothing would go in! When the meal was over, Mother took out everything that was in the drawer of the kitchen table – the bread, the cheese, the olives, etc. – and put it all up on the tray suspended from the ceiling, which I could not reach. She closed the barn door, put the plate with the beans in the drawer, and then said to me:

"Your plate is here until you make up your mind to eat. Until you eat the beans, you'll get nothing else."

I spent that afternoon ravenous with hunger. From time to time, I went into the kitchen and went to the table drawer, but there was nothing there except the plate of beans. I looked up at the tray where the bread with the cheese and olives was, but I couldn't reach. I went out to the yard, then down to the well, looking at the trees, but none of the fruit was yet ready to eat except for a few burs in the fork of the chestnut trees that had not been knocked down by the poles or the wind. I threw stones at them which, thank God, did not fall on my head but on the ground, leaving the chestnuts still lodged in the tree.

Evening came at last, and the time for supper. I was hoping that Mother would give me a dish of peas stewed with rice and rabbit, which is what we were having for supper, [but all she did was to] take the plate of beans out of the drawer, saying:

"Here you are, here's your plate. Until you eat your beans, you'll get nothing else.

I was very hungry, and also quite convinced that there was no way out, so I took hold of the plate and began to eat the beans. Then I noticed that my sisters were laughing, and in order not to see them laughing, I turned my back on them and began to eat facing the dresser. When I had eaten about half, my mother took the plate of beans away from me and gave me another plate with a helping of peas, rice and rabbit meat, saying:

"You have conquered your caprice, so now eat what the others are eating, and after that a bowlful of bread and curdled milk like the rest of us."

It was a lesson for a lifetime. I was never again tempted to say: "I won't eat this or that because I don't like it." At the time, I did not yet know about offering sacrifices to God, but He was preparing me. Thanks to Him and to the mother He chose for me.

20. Paying the price of curiosity

My mother used to put out corn meal for the hens towards the middle of the morning, and again in the afternoon. Sometimes she would send me to do this, and as soon as the hens heard me calling, they would come running, jumping and flying from the branches of the fig trees where they were perched. One day, I noticed that some of the hens, after eating the corn, went off. I went and said to my mother:

"Those hens are eating the meal and then they go off somewhere and don't lay their eggs here."

My mother replied:

"Don't you worry about the hens; let them go where they like."

But I was filled with curiosity and I wanted to know where the hens were going and what they were doing. The next day, I was on the watch, and when I saw them fly over the gate into the yard and set off down the path in the direction of the well, I went after them, and saw that they were going in under some brambles that were growing in a low retaining wall on the far side of the well, in front of which my father had some bee hives. Going in under the bramble bushes, first one, then another of the hens gradually disappeared. I got hold of a stick and started to poke about among the bushes in an attempt to part them so that I could see where the hens were and what they were doing. But what I saw was the bees buzzing round my face, stinging me all over. I struck out at them with the stick, and shaking them off I ran back home, calling out to my mother as I did so:

"Mother, help, the bees are trying to eat me!"

My mother came running. She drove off the bees that were still buzzing round my face, treated the stings, and then said :

"What were you up to? Messing about with the bees? Haven't I told you lots of times not to go near the hives? Come on now, you're alright!"

I replied:

"I didn't go near the bees. I only wanted to see where the hens were, and the bees got angry."

A few days later, I went back to the well, looking from a distance to see if a hen would appear. To my surprise, I saw one strutting along with a brood of chickens behind it, and picking at the ground to find something to eat. I dashed back to the house to get a piece of bread and crumbled it in front of the hen so that the chickens could eat it and I also put some water in an old dish I found there, and then I went to tell my mother:

"There's a hen with a brood of chickens down by the well, so I took a piece of bread and crumbled it up for them to eat.

My mother replied:

"Don't do that, pet! You must let them be hungry so that the hen will bring them up here to the yard in search of food. Once here, they'll stay."

Next morning, I went to see if the hen was out with her chickens and I met them underneath the chestnut trees, not far from the well, picking at the ground in among the parsley and violets that grew there in abundance. I broke off an olive branch and began to flap it at them to make them go up towards the yard. They went, slowly, behind the hen until they came to a small flight of stone steps which they had to climb in order to reach the yard. The hen flew up, but the chickens were not yet able to fly, so they remained at the bottom of the steps, cheeping. At that point, I wanted to get hold of them to place them at the top of the steps, but as soon as the mother hen saw me pick up the first one, she jumped down and flapped fiercely all round me, trying to peck at my hands. I began to run with the baby chicken in my hand, shouting:

"Mother, help, the hen is trying to peck me!"

My mother came when she heard me shouting. When she saw me with the chick in my hands and the hen flapping round me, she said:

"Let the chick go, let the chick go!"

So I threw the chick down on the ground. The mother hen then calmed down and led it back to the others, calling out to them.

My mother then went to get some rice and a dish with some clean water for them to eat and drink. After that, the mother hen settled down with the chicks under her wings. My mother then brought a basket with some straw in the bottom, grabbed hold of the hen and put her into it, covered with a sack; she then gathered up the chickens, put them in with the mother hen and brought them all up to the bakehouse, where she had already arranged some straw for them to sleep on in a corner close to the door. By the afternoon, they were already trotting in and out to the yard behind their mother, and happily eating and drinking. And there they stayed, with their mother.

A few days later, another hen appeared with an even larger brood of chicks, followed by another and yet another – I can't remember whether it was three or four. My mother gathered each of them up and took them to the yard, each one with her chicks. It was lovely to see so many little chicks eating and drinking, and running after their mothers, who tucked them in under their wings. I went very gently to make a fuss of them, but one of the hens flapped at my hands with her wings, which made me cry out for my mother, saying:

"Mother, this hen beat me. She's naughty! She's naughty!!"

"It's you that's being disobedient. Haven't I told you over and over again not to meddle either with the hens or with the chickens? Now the mother hen has punished you."

But I was sorely tempted to pick up one of the chicks and play with it.

21. Another act of Christian charity

When the chickens grew bigger, my sisters began to say:

"Oh, Mother, sell those chickens, they are eating such a lot of corn."

My mother replied :

"Let them be. They are only eating the corn and anything else that they are given. For the rest, they eat greens, grass, and fallen fruit. They take advantage of everything and at the same time clear things up. As long as there are chickens, we needn't kill any of the hens that are laying eggs.

On feast days my mother would sometimes kill one or two chickens and make a panful of chicken-broth large enough for the whole family to partake of, either for dinner or for supper. She cooked the meat, with some rice, in one or two glazed clay dishes which she then placed in the bread oven where they kept hot (provided the door of the oven was kept closed) until it was time to bring them to the table.

On these occasions, my mother used to send me to 'Uncle' Coxo's house, and also to that of an old lady who lived nearby [I have mentioned them in the Fifth Memoir, but I don't remember their names] to tell them not to cook anything for dinner (or for supper), depending on which meal my mother had made the broth for. So off I went, and they would give me the cans and the plates which I brought back home. Then, before she dished out the meal for the family, my mother used to put chicken and rice in those plates, cover them with another plate, and place them on top of the cans. These she would arrange in two baskets, which she had prepared beforehand with straw to preserve the heat, and she would send me to take everything to the people I mentioned. They would take the cans with the broth and the plates with the chicken and rice out of the baskets, say 'thank you', and settle down happily to enjoy their meal, while I ran back home with the baskets, but still arrived in time to eat with the rest of the family.

From time to time, people would come to my mother to ask if she had chickens to sell, because they had someone sick in the family who could not eat anything else. My mother would say yes. She would call to the hens with a little bit of corn and as they were eating, she would catch one of the chickens which she gave to the person who had asked.

They asked how much. If they were people who were able to pay, my mother would reply that the price was the current market price; if they were poor, and asked if we could wait for the money which at that moment they hadn't got but that they would bring it as soon as they had it, my mother would reply:

"Don't worry about having to pay. God will pay me. Take your chicken, and if you need any more, come and ask and God grant that the invalid may recover and will soon be well."

It seemed as if my mother knew those words of St Paul: «Each one must do as he has made up his mind, not reluctantly or under compulsion, for God loves a cheerful giver. And God is able to provide you with every blessing in abundance, so that you may always have enough of everything and may provide in abundance for every good work. As it is written, 'He scatters abroad, he gives to the poor, his righteousness endures for ever'» (II Cor. 9, 7-9)

Sometimes my mother used to pack a lot of little gifts into a little wicker basket we had in the house. [They used to tell me that I had come from heaven in it surrounded by roses and flowers.] Then she would send me to take them to various people who, she knew, were without those things. Sometimes it would be meat, when we killed a pig; at other times it would be traditional Christmas pastries (*filhoses*), etc., as I have already described in the Fifth Memoir. At other times it would be fruit, depending on what was in season: figs, apples, pears, cheeses that my mother made from the milk from our sheep. At other times, when they were available, it would be great bowlfuls of curdled milk which she took from the pans before processing the cheese, at the same time as she skimmed it off for the family. Then she would send me to take the things to various people for them to eat at supper with broken pieces of bread, which they greatly enjoyed and said 'thank you'.

When chestnuts were in season, it was a little basket of chestnuts, and when she sent me to take them to 'Uncle' Coxo's house, or to the old lady whom I have already mentioned several times, she told me to take a bundle of dry wood as well, so that they could light a fire and roast the chestnuts in the embers. She did this because the wood they had was damp and they had nowhere where they could keep it out of the rain. So off I went with the basket of chestnuts on my arm and the bundle of wood on my head.

22. A life of prayer

As I write this, I am reminded of the story of Abraham and [how] his son Isaac climbed the mountain carrying the bundle of wood destined for his own sacrifice though he did not realise this, and how God sent a ram to take his place in the holocaust, and made of [Abraham] the father of a great and countless progeny.

I, too, carried the wood, and God gave me, too, a great progeny, not according to nature, in flesh and blood, but according to grace: the blessing of God and the maternal protection of our heavenly Mother. So countless [is this progeny] that it is spread throughout the world from the farthest corners of which they stretch out their hands to me, imploring the blessing of God, the protection of Our Lady, healing for their ills, consolation in their distress, strength in their battles and light on their path. This is the progeny that God has given me, united with the bonds not of nature but in the Holy Spirit who dwells within us, as St Paul says:

«By one Spirit we were all baptised into one body – Jews or

Greeks, slaves or free – and all were made to drink of one Spirit» (I Cor. 12,13).

It is this Spirit which makes the whole earth, every human being, bear fruit; makes us, too, children of the same Father who is God everlasting, immense and immortal, and sharers in his immortality. This progeny is the generation of those who seek the Lord, and it is united in that same Spirit of faith, hope and love, that so many, from far away and from near at hand, pass through this humble abode, prolonging the echo of the voices of those who have gone before us, working, praying and singing, and now, in heaven, are singing the new hymn of thanksgiving and praise to the one God and true Saviour:

Our Father, who art in heaven, hallowed be thy name,
Thy kingdom come, thy will be done on earth as it is in heaven.
Give us this day our daily bread,
And forgive us our trespasses,
as we forgive those who trespass against us,
And lead us not into temptation, but deliver us from evil.

Hail Mary, full of grace, the Lord is with thee;
Blessed art thou among women,
And blessed is the fruit of thy womb, Jesus.
Holy Mary, Mother of God, pray for us, sinners,
Now and at the hour of our death. Amen.

Glory be to the Father and to the Son and to the Holy Spirit.
As it was in the beginning, is now and ever shall be,
world without end, Amen.

We seek God, ungrateful as we are,
The supreme Father, the Redeemer,
They make fun of the faith, foolish people
They rebel in vain against the Lord

Bless, O holy Virgin,
The expression of our faith.
We want God for our King
We want God for our Father!

> We seek God! O gentle Mother,
> An afflicted people comes re-echoing
> At your feet this cry from the heart
> Which you will carry to the feet of God.
>
> We seek God! And we intend
> His holy law to defend!
> We promise here to serve Him always
> We seek God until we die!

That is how the days, months and years were spent in this humble home, in quiet peace and joy, smiling at the future of the young people as they blossomed with the sweet-scented smell of the freshest rosebuds that bloomed every day in the climbing roses that decorated the walls of our house.

During the month of May, we used to recite the Rosary as a family every day. It was my mother who used to give it out, at night, after supper, and grace after supper which my father used to start, in the front room, kneeling before a Crucifix that hung there.

At the end of each mystery we used to sing a verse of a hymn to Our Lady:

> Hail holy Patron
> Of the people you protect,
> Chosen from among all
> To be God's people.
>
> O Glory of our land
> Which you have saved a thousand times
> As long as the People of Portugal exist
> You will be loved by them.
>
> Sweet-smelling flower!
> For every Portuguese heart!
> Amongst us, in every believer
> You have a perfect devotee.
>
> You are the most perfect work
> That came from the hands of God!
> There is no greater creature
> In heaven or on earth!

To help us is your glory!
You have no greater joy:
No-one calls on Mary
And is left unaided.

You are our Patron!
Do not cease your care
Of the flock
That has been entrusted to your care.

Portugal, like a second phoenix,
Comes to life again.
Let no-one claim to be Portuguese
Who does not profess the Christian faith.

Many other people came to join us: from Aljustrel, Casa Velha, Eira de Pedra, Fatima, Lomba d'Egua and Moita. Sometimes there were so many people that they could not all fit inside the house, which was small, so they would remain outside in the street and in the courtyard, joining their voices to ours, praying and singing the praises of God and Our Lady, and asking for their blessing and protection.

24. "They all want to perch on the roost"

At that time, May devotions were not held in the parish church. Only much later was the parish priest able to begin holding them, probably because we were in the early years of the Republic during which the Church suffered a good deal of persecution, the practice of religion had to be restricted and hidden, the churches were kept shut, it was forbidden to hold processions, or to ring the church bells, while priests were arrested, and male and female religious were expelled from the country, and so on.

In Fatima, the persecution was not quite so severe, possibly because it was off the beaten track and almost unknown; but even so the parish priest had to tread very carefully.

My mother never appeared to be afraid. We lived our lives tranquilly and little was said in our house about the situation. I do however remember having occasionally heard my mother speak regretfully of the death of the king and the young prince; and at night, when my father was leading the grace, she would suggest to him that we should say an Our Father for the eternal repose of the king and the prince. If people who came to the house did happen to speak about these things, my mother used to say that the rich are like cocks. They all want to perch on the roost and give orders, and so they went about killing one another, closing the churches and forbidding people to go there to pray; moreover they preach false doctrines which they themselves have invented to deceive the people. "But we have faith and we know that God exists, we know the commandments of God's law and of Holy Mother Church, that this is what we have to do, and that is where we have to go, whether they like it or not. And the worst of it is that they come here looking for our sons to send them to their deaths in those wars they start, though our sons are perfectly innocent! God help us!"

24. Household tasks

With this attitude, my mother went on with her life of faithful spouse, mother and housewife, praying, and doing as many good deeds as she could.

In the afternoons, my mother used to take some of the milk that was taken from the flock when they returned from pasture, put it in a container and give it to me to take to some sick person who my mother knew had none, so that they could drink it at bedtime. [She would also send me] to 'Uncle' Coxo and the old lady I have already mentioned several times. When they could, these people used to come up to our house to say 'thank you', and to ask if there was any little job that my mother wanted done that they could do, and so be a help to us. To please them, my mother always said 'yes'. In 'Uncle' Coxo's case, and if the weather was fine, she would ask him to mince young cabbages small enough for the hens to eat. Then he would sit on a bench in the shade of the fig trees with a huge basket of cabbages on one side and a wooden bowl in front of him into which he was to mince the cabbages. But not many fell into the bowl because the hens used to come and jump all round him, grabbing the pieces of cabbage and flying off with them hanging from their mouths, in an effort to escape from their companions, who ran after them trying to pull the pieces from them. When he had finished this task, if there were any dry broad beans, peas, haricot beans, lupins or such like on the threshing floor to be de-podded and the seeds cleaned in readiness for the next sowing, he went there, whistling cheerfully. There he would spend the afternoon happily, being entertained by the children who played and jumped about all round him.

In the case of the old lady, if there were children in the cots, my mother would ask her to sit down on a stool near them and rock the cradles to make them go to sleep, and to put their dummy in their mouth for them to suck, and so prevent them from crying. My mother used to say that this helped her a lot as I would then be free to keep an eye on the older children, playing with them, and also going on messages. If there were no babies, my mother used to ask the old lady to sit down near the winder in order to fill the shuttles for the loom, and so be a help to my sister Maria dos Anjos as well.

When the sheep were being sheared, they would come and help us to open the wool after it had been washed, getting it ready to be put into fine folders when the carders came, and then sent to the factory to be spun and dyed in the various colours my mother asked for. After this, she would make warm wraps for the winter.

The two old people thus spent happy afternoons, and at night would have supper with us, join in the grace after meals that my father recited, and then go off home, taking with them a little can of milk which my mother would give them to take before going to bed, to make sure they would have a good night's sleep.

Whenever, now, I recite Psalm 127, it seems to me that what the psalmist says can well be applied to my parents:

> "O blessed are you who fear the Lord
> and walk in his ways.
> By the labour of your hands you shall eat,
> you shall be happy and prosper;
> your wife like a fruitful vine
> in the heart of your house;
> your children like shoots of the olive,
> around your table.
> Indeed thus shall be blessed
> the man who fears the Lord.
> May the Lord bless you from Sion
> all the days of your life!

May you see your children's children
in a happy Jerusalem!
On Israel peace! (Psalm 127, 1-6).

25. The story of the fox

My mother was cheerful and outgoing in temperament. She loved to tell amusing stories about my childish escapades. I did not always like this, and used to say that my mother was making fun of me. My mother used to reply:

"No, I'm not making fun of you; it's just to show how clever and intelligent you are."

This reply satisfied me as I thought it was the truth. It was self-love, which manifests itself very soon after people are born.

Two of the episodes she liked to recount occurred when I was four or five years old. There was a family in Vila Nova de Ourém who were friends of ours, I'm not quite sure why. It consisted of two unmarried sisters, known as the Guimaroas, who kept a draper's shop facing the church, on the opposite side of the street. There was also a gentleman known as Senhor Guimarães. Whenever my father went into the town, if he had any game (rabbits, hares, partridges, etc.) he would take some to them as a present, which they greatly appreciated.

One day, Sr. Guimarães asked my father if he could get him a live fox. My father said he would see, because it did sometimes happen that foxes, too, got caught in his snares. My father usually killed the foxes and then sold the skin. However, he used to bury the rest as people said that fox meat was not good to eat. Shortly afterwards, my father trapped a very fine and quite large fox. The first opportunity he got to go to Vila Nova de Ourem to sell things – it was my father who used to sell the produce from Godmother Teresa's land together with what was left over from our own after feeding the family and the animals – he made up a cart-load, put the side flaps on the cart, put the fox into a wooden cage – which he already had for transporting animals – and put it onto the cart in among the rest of the things he was taking. He then told me to sit on top of the cage, and off we went.

The fox was jumping about so much in the cage that it nearly sent me flying, until it did, in fact, manage to reach out from the cage with its front paws and snatch part of the hem of my dress, which it tore to pieces with its nails and teeth. I began to call out:

"Papa, the fox is going to eat me!"

My father took no notice and just said calmly :

"Keep still and relax, the fox will do you no harm!"

But the fox kept pulling more and more of my dress into the cage. As I felt myself more and more firmly held, I called out:

"Papa, the fox really is going to eat me!"

"Keep still, little one, the fox will do you no harm."

"But it is, it is going to eat me, it is, it is!"

I shouted so much that my father stopped the cart and came round to see. He pulled the pieces of my dress out of the cage, and looked carefully to see whether the fox had scratched my legs. Fortunately not, as I had stuck them out in front of me. Then he told me to go and sit on a sack of potatoes, and on we went. When we reached the town, he went immediately to deliver the fox to Sr. Guimarães, who lived in a tall house beside the church, before you come to the street that leads down, on the right, to "Fish Square". When Sr. Guimarães saw the fox, he was delighted. It was handsome as well as being both alert and wild. He at once called to his wife to come and have a look at it. She came, and when she had looked at the fox and admired it, she greeted my father and then came to give me a kiss, which is when she noticed the state of my dress. She asked what had happened. My father explained that the fox had done it. Then she went to look for a dress – which I imagine must have belonged to one of her daughters – and put it on me. It fitted me well. They invited my father to have lunch with them. At first my father thanked them but said 'no', as he had to go down to the square and sell some things that he had brought with him, but they were so insistent that in the end he had no choice but to accept, so as soon as my father finished his business in the square, we went there. My father used to say that he did not like to accept these invitations as he was not accustomed to eating at the same table with grandees.

After the meal, we said goodbye to them and returned home as evening was drawing in. When my mother saw me, she asked my father why he had gone to one of the gentry to buy me a new dress! My father replied by handing her the dress I had been wearing and telling her to look and see what the fox had done. When my mother saw it, she asked:

"And didn't it scratch the little one's legs?"

"No, it didn't", my father replied, "because she stuck them out in front of her".

Then my mother laughed and hung the dress on the beams of the loom for everyone to see what the fox had done, and there it stayed until my sister Teresa took it and mended it, by putting an entirely new piece to it, from the waist down. ([I should explain that] children up to the age of about seven used to wear dresses; only from the age of about seven onwards did they begin to wear blouses and skirts; this explains why in some of the photographs, the Ven. Jacinta is wearing a dress and in others a blouse and skirt.)

26. The fruits of the Holy Spirit

The other episode that my mother used to relate laughingly was how, one day, I had overheard her asking my father what there was on the land ready to eat, and his reply:

"The fruits of the Holy Spirit [i.e. The fruits that will be ready for Pentecost (Translator)] are broad beans, peas and cherries."

I kept this reply in my head and when, on Sunday, after Mass, the parish priest was teaching catechism to the children, he asked:

"Now, then, children, can any of you tell me which are the fruits of the Holy Spirit?"

I promptly stood up and said:

"I know, I know".

"Do you now?" replied the parish priest. "What are they then?"

"Broad beans, peas and cherries."

I was very surprised when I saw the parish priest laughing, as well as my mother and all the people who were in the church listening to the catechism lesson while they waited to take their children home when the lesson was over. Then the parish priest asked me:

"And who taught you that, little one?"

"I heard my father say it to my mother."

Then my mother stood up and explained what had happened.

When, later, we were having our dinner at home, my mother told my father what had happened and my father replied, laughingly:

"It wasn't entirely wrong, as these are the fruits of the earth through the Holy Spirit."

When my father said this, I plucked up courage and said:

"So you see, mother, what I said was right".

But my mother replied :

"No, you gave a list of the fruits of the earth, whereas the parish priest asked you what were the fruits of the Holy Spirit, which are different: they are charity, joy, peace, longanimity, meekness, faith, modesty, continence and chastity, patience, benignity and goodness." And she set about teaching them to me there and then, so that the next time I should be able to say what they were.

27. Sunday afternoons

As I have already said in the Fifth Memoir, on Sundays and Holidays of Obligation, my father used to spend the afternoon playing cards in our yard with some of his friends. As they played, they had a jug of wine in front of them so that they could drink a glassful between rounds. In the summer, my mother, very cleverly, used to prepare a cool drink in a large jug, made of honey, lemon juice and cold water which she would have gone to fetch from the well for the purpose (my parents had two lemon trees in the corner on the left formed by the two earth walls supporting our own yard and Godmother Teresa's as you go down from the yard towards the well). She would then place the jug on the table in front of the men, together with a large glazed earthenware plate with fruit, saying cheerfully :

"Here's some fruit for you all to eat and a nice cold drink; the more wine you drink, the hotter you'll be." Then she would unobtrusively pick up the jug of wine and take it away. They would say 'thank you' and be satisfied.

In the winter they used to play in the open shed, and then it was with pots of coffee and plates of dried figs or roast chestnuts that she made herself liked and welcome.

Sometimes, they would invite my mother to join their game. She would agree, because she was very good at it, and nearly always won. Then she would suggest that each one should put a *tostão* (a very small coin) in the middle of the table, saying:

"If I lose a *tostão,* it's not a lot; if I win, I'll win quite a few."

At the end, when she did win, which was nearly always, she would gather up all the coins and put them in the pocket of her apron saying:

"Thanks be to God! Now, tomorrow, I can send and buy a few boxes of matches, some spools of thread and a length of cloth."

Then, smiling, she would go off to spend the rest of the afternoon with the aunts and other neighbours, talking to them, as they sat either in the yard with their backs against the wall of the sheep pen, or else in the front room, if it was cold or wet; at other times they would sit on the steps leading up to our house from the road, from where they could keep an eye on the children as they played, running up and down the road, sometimes competing for five or ten *reis* (an even smaller coin), which each one would have placed on the top of a low wall at the far end, like a little island between the two streets. After we had all gone there to put our coin on the top of the wall, we used to line up in a row in front of our house and: 'one, two, three,' we all set off running. And the first to get there won all those coins. Some of the children would fall and then their mothers would come along to dust the pebbles off their knees, and tend to any cuts or scratches.

That was how we spent happy afternoons, after we had been to Holy Mass in the morning, in order to fulfil the Sunday precept and the other duties of each one's state, until the church bell rang [for the Angelus]. When all had recited the Hail Mary's that were led by my father, they would all say goodbye and go off, each one with her husband and children, to their own homes, with a tranquil conscience at the end of a Lord's day well spent, to have supper and have a good rest in preparation for the next day when they would get up at sunrise and work until sunset.

My mother used to say farewell to each and all, cheerful and smiling, and saying:

"Goodbye, until tomorrow, or, until next Sunday, God willing."

She used to say the same to my sisters' boyfriends and those of the other young girls, who used to come to spend their afternoons in our house, talking to their boyfriends, in pairs, spread out under the shade of the fig trees, within sight of their parents who were playing at the front. Their quiet conversations were interrupted by the ringing of the Angelus. With uncovered head, they would respond to the Hail Mary with everyone else, then, with a wave of the hand to their girl friends and to my parents, they would say "goodbye, until next Sunday, God willing". Then they would go off, some whistling, others singing, playing the mouth organ or strumming the strings of their guitar as they set off on their way: the one who later married my sister Maria dos Anjos in the direction of Boleiros as far as the Currais; another went over the mountain of *Nossa Senhora da Ortiga* as far as Lomba, which is where the one who married my sister Teresa came from; another headed in the direction of Santa Catarina as far as Chainça, which is where the one who married my sister Gloria came from; while the one who married my sister Carolina went to Casa Velha.

When the weather was fine, we next had to take back to the threshing floor the trestles, with the side of the cart which had done duty as a table for the card players. We then went to the kitchen to get the salad bowls with lettuce, tomato or green bean salad; to the ovens to get the big glazed pottery roasting pans with the meat and roast potatoes, or peas with rice, etc., or whatever the supper dish was, and everything was ready for us to have a good supper out in the fresh air from the Serra bearing the scent of the eucalyptus, the olive and pine trees that crowned the mountain in front of us.

And there Godmother Teresa and the rest of her household would join us, when she had been invited to do so, – though Godfather Anastácio would already be there, since he was one of the men who used to come and spend the afternoons on Sundays and Holidays of Obligation playing cards in our yard. Godmother would always bring something extra to enhance the celebration: flasks of white whine, little baskets of fritters or some choice fruit, or bowls with *bailhoses* (a kind of fritter) in syrup.

The only one missing was my brother Manuel, and already in the distance one could hear the sound of his harmonica as he crossed the mountain of *Nossa Senhora da Ortiga* from the direction of Ramila where he had spent the afternoon with his fiancée, Emilia, whom he married in the Fatima parish church to which they both belonged. God blessed their marriage with 11 children, whom they brought up and educated as good Christians.

Supper was a quiet and cheerful meal, in peace and contentment. Each one told of their adventures or experiences, and then everyone laughed or made comments, each in their own way, without argument. Sometimes, Aunt Olimpia with all her household would also join us, though not very often as there were a great many of them and when they all came, there was almost no room on the threshing floor, and sometimes also because Uncle Marto's ways of thinking and being were different from those of my parents. But when they did come, the one who enjoyed the celebration most of all was little Jacinta, who used to sit next to me at supper. Afterwards, no-one could persuade her to go back to her own house. She would cling on to me, saying:

"I'm staying here with you".

The same thing used to happen even on other days when she came to spend the afternoon playing with me in our yard. On these occasions, my mother used to say to her father or mother:

"If she doesn't want to go, let her stay; they'll both fit in the one bed and there's enough supper for all."

Thus, life went on in our house, in peace, joy and serenity, with no worries other than those connected with our humble work from day to day, which each one performed in accordance with our parents' wishes, without complaints or arguments. My father was responsible for the work in the fields, while my mother looked after the house. Together they decided what it was best for each one to do, and were always in agreement.

Whenever necessary, my two older sisters, Maria and Teresa, used to go and help with the work in the fields. My mother never made any objection, however much weaving and sewing work there was to do in the house, though at times there was a lot. When they were preparing wedding trousseaus, the materials had to be woven on the loom, linen for sheets, blankets for the beds, etc.; then, in the case of the dressmaking, it was Teresa who did the finishing, cutting out, making the sheets, pillow cases, towels, clothes, etc. Faced with all this, my mother used to say:

"It doesn't matter. The first thing is to help Father with the work in the fields, then we will all help with these things in the evening, and everything will get done with the help of God." And so it was: God did indeed always came to our aid.

28. *Calvary*

At that time, no-one had the remotest idea of the great cross that God had in store for my mother to carry up the steep hill of her own particular Calvary.

It began with a sad episode that turned all the people of the parish against the parish priest.

My father, who was a peaceable man, did not wish to get involved. However, he was so shocked by what had happened that he ceased to go [to the parish church] to make his Easter duty with his family once a year, as the custom was. He did not stop carrying out all his other duties as a Christian, such as going to Mass on Sundays and Holidays. Moreover, he used to take advantage of his visits to Vila Nova de Ourém to go to confession [there] from time to time, as well as going every year to the celebrations for the Feast of Our Lady of Ortiga – where a number of priests used to come from other places to help with the confessions – in order to go to confession and Communion and so gain the Jubilee indulgence. This pacified my mother to some extent, but not entirely, as she felt that although to make one's Easter duty in one's own parish church was not a binding obligation – and nowadays, I understand, the custom * has been abandoned – she was never entirely reconciled to the situation and did everything in her power to help my father to get over this difficulty. When she did not succeed, she used to bemoan the fact, saying:

"I still haven't managed to win this grace from God. It must be because of my sins, because we are all sinners and we have to be patient."

And so the time passed until my two older sisters, Maria and Teresa, had their boyfriends or fiancés, I'm not sure which, and were thinking of getting married.

Then my mother and father decided that my other two sisters, Gloria and Carolina, should learn to weave and do dressmaking

---

* *The custom was for the entire family to go in a body to the parish Church on an appointed day in order to make their annual Confession. Each one's name was then ticked or marked off in a book in some way. The parish priest thus knew exactly who had and who hadn't 'fulfilled his/her obligation'. (Translator's note)*

and help with the work in the fields, in order to take over from my two older sisters when they got married.

For this to happen, it would be necessary for me, then aged seven but going on for eight, to take over from Caroline who, until then, had always taken our flock of sheep out to pasture.

29. *"Our house began to be much less lively"*

This change meant that our house began to be much less lively. The children who used to come and play in our yard stopped coming; just a few of them used to wait for me in the evenings when I returned from pasturing the sheep, in order to go with me to the threshing floor and watch out for Our Lady and the Angels to come and light their lamps and place them in the windows of heaven to light the way for us, or else to run up and down the road, chasing the fireflies and calling out:

> Little light, little light
> Where are you going ?
> Come and light the fire,
> The rice is not yet cooked.

My mother felt deeply the absence of the children in our house, as she was so accustomed to their company, and to giving a slice of bread and cheese to any of them who said they were hungry; to the smaller ones she used to give a cup of milk with broken pieces of bread, and to the babies, just milk. When they were plentiful, she used to put out on the threshing floor, or under the shade of the fig trees small baskets containing fruit, figs, apples, pears or, when they were in season, chestnuts or sweet acorns that had been stewed or roasted, for the children to amuse themselves shelling and eating them.

When she was teaching catechism to all these children, she used to place all the babies' cradles, if there were any, near her so that she could at the same time rock them and put the dummy in their mouths so that they did not cry. She used to tie a piece of string across the cradle with a little bell in the middle, so that the baby could reach out and touch and shake it with its fingers and so amuse itself by hearing it ring. Or again, she would put a tiny sprig of rosemary or basil, a carnation or a rose which, when shaken, would let its petals fall onto the cradle so that the child could smell the delicate perfume of these flowers while at the same time being amused.

My mother used to tell a story about a woman who had given birth to a baby, but had no milk to feed it, so she accustomed the child to suck from a goat. The animal got so fond of the child that when it was time for the baby to feed, the goat used to escape from the pasture and come running to the house. Then, placing one of its hind legs across the cradle, it would place itself in the right position for the child to feed, and the baby grew into a fine child, much stronger than many others.

At the end of the story, my mother used to say:

"What a fine example for those fathers and mothers who abandon their children, and even deprive them of life. Animals have a greater love for their young, and even for those who are not their own, than these heartless men and women!"

Yet at that time, such cases were relatively rare. What would my mother say if she were alive today when such things are done with the greatest of indifference, in cold blood, almost like drinking a glass of cold water.

The times may have changed for the worse, but the Law of God has not changed nor will it change, not one jot or one tittle is to be omitted from the Law: "Thou shalt not kill".

30. The Story of a Princess

Sometimes my mother used to entertain the children by telling them stories while they sat on the ground round her wide-eyed, with their eyes shining like pearls as they listened motionless. Here is one of the stories she used to tell:

There was a princess who lived in a great palace with her ladies and servants. She had immense grounds with a lovely garden, and lakes of sparkling water where she used to bathe every day. There were lots of lovely birds of every kind which used to sing beautifully: peacocks with magnificent tails which flew around, carrier pigeons which carried her messages wherever she wished, and talking parrots which came and told the princess all that was going on in the world.

One day, the princess called one of the parrots and told it to go to other lands to see what was happening there, and then come back and tell her.

The parrot went, and came back to tell the princess that it had seen vast lands, where there were many wars and men were killing one another, with blood in the streets and many people lying wounded on the ground, groaning and unable to get up as there was no-one to look after them; many dead people, too were lying there on the ground as there was no-one to bury them.

Then the princess sent another parrot, and told it to go to other lands, and then come back and tell her what it had seen. The parrot went and returned to tell the princess that it had seen a great many old people who had been abandoned, and were starving and freezing, with nothing to eat or wear, and nobody to look after them. The depths of distress!

Then the princess sent yet another parrot to see what was happening in the great wide world. It went and came back to tell the princess that it had seen a whole lot of children who had been abandoned, crying with cold and hunger, with no-one to take care of them.

Whereupon the princess sent for all the menservants in her palace and told them to go with the parrot who had seen the old people and bring them all to live in her palace and take care of them so that they should not need anything until the day that God came to take them to heaven.

After that, she summoned all her maidservants and told them to go with the parrot who had seen all the abandoned children and to bring them, too, to her palace, give them all they needed and teach them to know, love and serve God and to work in order to earn their daily bread until they were settled in life.

Some people went and told the King, who was the princess's father, what she had done, and he said:

"Clearly, my daughter has a vocation to marry and have lots of children who will be my heirs. Let us go and look for a Prince for her to marry."

So he went to other lands until he found a prince whom he brought and presented to the princess, saying:

"Here is a prince to marry you, my daughter, and may God bless you and give you many children who will be our heirs and the future of our country."

The princess looked at the prince and said:

" No, father. I'm not going to marry him."

"Why not?" asked the King.

"Because he is lame," the princess replied.

This made the king sad, but he went off again to other lands in search of another prince to come and marry the princess. When he had found one he brought him to the princess and said:

"Now, here is a prince to marry you. He is not lame; he walks well."

The princess looked at the prince and said:

"No! I won't marry this one either".

"Why not?" the king asked.

"Because he's a hunchback." she replied.

The king was angered by this and he said:

"I am going to punish the princess. She must get married, even if it is to a peasant."

But the courtiers said to the king:

"There, in that other country, there is yet another prince. Perhaps the princess will agree to marry him."

So the king sent his servants to look for the prince and bring him to the princess, but when she saw him she said:

"No, I won't marry him either."

"And why not? asked the king.

"Because he's cross-eyed."

The king was furious. But he knew that nearby there was a festival to which a great many young men went. So he went there and after looking on for some time, he saw a young man that he liked the look of. So he called him and said to him:

"Come with me and marry the princess."

But the young man refused, saying:

"My Lord King, I am not the man you want, nor am I thinking of marrying. I am poor, I only have a little house where I live, and a little carpenter's shop where I earn enough to live on from day to day, but not enough to keep a family; for this reason, I intend to go on as I am.

But the king insisted and the young man gave in and went with him. The king brought him to the princess and said to her:

"Now, you must marry this one".

She looked at the young man and said:

"Yes. I will marry this one. He is honest, pure and chaste, pious and hard-working, and he will respect the vow of chastity by which I dedicated myself to God."

And she left her palace in the care of her menservants and maidservants, for them to look after the old people and the children, and she married the young man, and they went to live in a poor little house in a small village, where they worked to gain their daily bread.

Later on, God sent them from heaven the Child Jesus for them to bring up and educate so that, when he was grown up, he could die on the cross to save all of us who are sinners.

This princess was Our Lady. The pure and chaste young man who married her was St Joseph, and the king, her father, was the prophet David who had been a great sinner. When he had repented, he begged God's pardon, did penance, and is now the holy king David.

This was the kind of story that my mother used to tell to the children to entertain them; they all had a deep moral meaning designed to instil faith, hope and charity into the children.

31. The gift of life

My mother used to say that children come to prolong the lives of those who give them their physical being, that they were like plants that, placed in the earth as seeds, burst forth with new life, clothed with fresh foliage and strength, yielding flowers and fruits of all kinds, enriching the earth and filling it with delicate scents and perfumes. That's what children are like with the grace and candour of their innocence, as are pure and chaste young people, smiling at the tomorrow that is approaching like a new garden, where fresh smiling rosebuds are bursting into bloom.

Here I recall what Scripture says: "How lovely are the smiles of innocence and of pure hearts: God takes his delight in them."

It was in this spirit that my mother, following the example and in the footsteps of Aunt Isabel, used to take in abandoned children, those born to unmarried mothers whose own parents often treated them badly, refusing to accept the fruit of their sin and treating them as the greatest shame to fall upon their household.

As a result these young girls found themselves shamed, deprived of support, with no where to go. Repentant and ashamed, they used to come and knock on our door to see what Aunt Maria Rosa would say to them and what they were to do. My mother always received them kindly with an understanding of human frailty; she used to help and support them, tell them what they should do and encourage them, telling them that if, afterwards, their parents refused to accept the babies that would be born, she would take them and look after them until their parents agreed to let the babies' mothers bring them home, or some good family were found to adopt them.

As an example of all this, I will describe here what happened to a young inexperienced girl, aged 15 or 16, who lived in Casa Velha, the first village beyond Aljustrel, because this particular case shows the great value my mother attached to the gift of life, in the light of the commandments of God's Law "Thou shalt not kill". It also shows the lengths to which she would go to in the practice of charity.

The events I describe took place before I myself was born. I got to know about them from hearing them talked about many years later, and I knew all the people involved.

At the time there was a doctor, who was also a surgeon, who used to come to Aljustrel and the surrounding area on certain days in order to see patients. Some of them used to wait for him in our house, which is where he saw them, and my mother was the one who did the dressings, administered the medicine, etc., for those who had no-one at home who could do this for them. Others used to wait for the doctor at the door of their own home, in order to consult him as he passed. The young girl I refer to did precisely this. He accordingly dismounted, tethered his horse to the trunk of one of the olive trees near the house and went inside, where he took advantage of the situation to violate her.

When, later, the girl's father and her brothers learnt what had happened, they were up in arms against the doctor and waited for the first opportunity to catch him and set upon him. He, out of fear, stopped coming. He used to come only as far as S. Mamede, and anyone who wanted to consult him had to go there.

Faced with an atmosphere of hostility in her own family circle, and feeling herself looked upon as a shame and disgrace to the family, the poor girl was very unhappy.

Sad and depressed, she came to see my mother and ask her what she ought to do.

My mother received her with kindness and understanding, and advised her to ask her father to allow her to come to our house to learn dressmaking with my sister Teresa. Her father agreed to this, so she spent her days in our house but went back to her father's house at night to sleep. In this way, my mother was able to keep an eye on her and support her.

When the child was born, the girl's father said he did not want the child in the house. Because of this, she used to look after it and feed it in our house during the day. At night the child stayed with my mother, while the girl went back to her father's house to sleep. This went on until her father at last resolved to allow her to bring the child home with her. My mother used to say that she had acted as she did in order to prevent the girl from leaving home or abandoning the child.

When, later, God gave me the gift of life and I grew up, I came to know the little boy who used to come with all the others to play with me in our yard – as far as I remember I must have been about four or five at the time. The boy was known as 'Carvalhico'.

One day he came to our house in floods of tears. I asked him why he was crying. He said he was crying because his grand-father and his uncles didn't like him, and that they were always scolding him and beating him. I asked where was his father, but he said he had none.

"But you have a grandfather", I replied, "whereas I have a father, but no grandfather!"

Without understanding the real state of affairs, I went and told my mother that Carvalhico was crying and saying that he had no father but that he did have a grandfather, whereas I had a father but no grandfather (I never knew either of my grandfathers). My mother explained:

"God arranges these things. To some he gives a father, to others a grandfather, to some he gives a horse and a donkey, to others neither a horse nor a donkey so they have to walk."

I went to console Carvalhico with this reply, telling him that God had arranged things like that: that he gave a horse and a donkey to some people, and neither horse nor donkey to others so that they had to walk.

At night, when my father came home and we were having supper, I told my father what my mother had said (that God gives some people a father, to others he gives a grandfather, to some he gives a horse and a donkey and to other neither horse nor donkey) and I asked him why things were like that:

My father replied:

"It's because these people don't know how to ride a horse and as soon as they sit on a donkey's back they fall off, but when you are bigger I will teach you to ride so that you won't fall off."

Years later, that child married my sister Carolina. He was a good Christian, a practising Catholic, a good husband and worker, cultivating his own land and in this way providing for his wife and family by the sweat of his brow and the help of God. They settled in the house belonging to his grandfather which he inherited, and to which he made some alterations. God granted him the grace of giving one of his sons to the Church as a priest and a daughter as a religious sister. I have already referred to these in listing my sister Carolina's descendants.

One day, a neighbour of ours who lived almost opposite our house – she was my godmother's mother – said to my mother that she did not know how my mother could bear to receive into her house all the human wretchedness that came knocking at our door. My mother replied:

"Look! What do we do when we see someone fall down. Don't we run at once to give them a hand to help them up, and then support them so that they won't fall again? Well, that's what I do. I give a helping hand so that someone who has fallen once won't fall again. When he was on earth, Jesus Christ welcomed the repentant Magdalen who had been a great sinner, and he forgave her. He received the woman taken in adultery, whom all those old men wanted to stone to death, and he forgave her, telling her not to sin again. That is what I try to do: to forgive, and to help the person not to fall back into the wretchedness of sin, to keep the commandments of God's Law, which oblige us to be chaste.

32. From the festival to the desert

We have already referred to the first two steps which my mother had to climb up the hill of her Calvary. [I mean] the beginning of the crisis that my father went through towards the end of his life, when she did everything she could to help him to get over it and not cease to fulfil his religious duties, and the beginning of my life as a shepherdess, as a result of which our house began to be less lively, with the loss of the liveliness of the children who used to come and spend the day there playing with me, something which my mother much enjoyed, though it also created work and made her tired. But, as St Paul says: charity is cheerful, it runs and does not delay.

The third step up the slope of her Calvary was the marriage of my two older sisters, Maria and Teresa. The gap that they left in our house was not due solely to their absence, but to the absence, also, of the young girls who used to come there to learn weaving and dress-making with them. [Once my sisters had married and left home], these, too, no longer came. My sisters Gloria and Carolina had learned to take their places when they got married, but they lacked the skill, and they much preferred the outside life, going out to help Father in the fields and being with the workers at the time of the vintage and olive gathering.

Thus, during the day, my mother was alone in the house, which was as empty as a desert, and she felt very lonely. She sometimes used to say:

"I don't know how it is, but it seems to me that we have gone from a festival to the desert."

Neither she nor anyone else could foresee that maybe God himself was emptying that house so that before long it would be occupied by people of a different kind, almost like an unending queue which, for her, would be yet another enormous slope she would have to negotiate to reach the top of her Calvary.

Maria settled nearby, almost opposite our own house, but Teresa went to live a long way away. Only on Sundays and Holidays of Obligation did she come with her husband to Mass in the parish church, after which they used to come and eat at our house with all the family. Then, at the end of the afternoon, after the afternoon snack, she and her husband would go back home, crossing the hill of Our Lady of Ortiga, pausing for a blessing as they trudged past her little chapel on their way back to Lomba where they lived.

The next day, early in the morning, my father and my brother with Gloria and Carolina would set off for their work in the fields. I went out to pasture the sheep and my mother remained on her own in the empty house.

Occasionally, a neighbour would call to ask for something that she needed: to borrow a loaf of bread because her own was used up before the day on which she made a new batch; or a pitcher of water, because her storage tank was empty and it was such a long way to Fonte Nova; some onions because she had used up all her own and the new crop was still out in the ground and only half grown, so it would be a shame to pull them up, etc. My mother received them all smilingly, with pleasure and satisfaction.

People used to come from all sides to ask her to go and take care of someone who was sick, but she now had no-one to whom she could entrust the housework, so she used to call on my sister Maria. She would go to her house and call her, and ask her to come over to our house to prepare the dinner, or the supper, and to make enough for everyone, asking both herself and her husband to come and eat dinner or supper in our house, to look after the animals and, when my father returned, to tell him where she had gone.

And so each work-filled day went by, with my mother praying and singing, but now there was only her own melodious voice to be heard, and how she missed the childish treble of the little ones who used to be all round her; she missed, too, the voices of her daughters and the other young people who used to join in. But she used to say: "That's life; everything comes to an end. Only God remains the same!" Her faith was her consolation and God her support.

It was as if she knew Psalm 39, and prayed and sang it:

"I waited, I waited for the Lord and he stooped down to me.
He set my feet upon a rock and made my footsteps firm.
He put a new song into my mouth praise of our God."

Yes, she sang now in a different way, and God was to ask of her much more than she knew or dreamt of: it would be the most difficult step she had to negotiate in mounting her Calvary. It was the same for her as for Our Lady, to whom the Incarnation of the Son of God brought difficulties, anxieties, sorrows, anguish and martyrdom – St Joseph's doubts, the persecution that forced her to leave her home and country to take refuge in a foreign country; after her return, the contradictions and plots of those who sought to kill her Son. That is how it is: where God is, the devil appears, stirring up conflicts, battles and contradictions. All these things are a sign of the presence of God. If they did not come from God, the devil would have nothing to fear as he would not be in danger of losing his domain.

33. Apparitions are children's tales ...

Then the apparitions happened. To begin with, my mother attached no importance to them: children invent such things, who is going to take any notice? At the same time, she was careful to warn me not to make up stories or to tell lies and deceive people, and she used to scold me because she thought the whole thing was a lie.

But the situation got progressively worse. After the first apparition of Our Lady on 13th May, 1917 the news spread rapidly and people began to gather round, coming to our house to ask what had happened, what it was all about, what it was that people were saying that the children had seen, and so on.

My mother tried to undeceive them all :

"Don't take any notice of it. It is all children's talk. What I don't know is how it came into their heads to say such a thing! And it's incredible that people actually believe them! How can it be? God help me! I could have done without all this!"

When I returned with the sheep at night, my mother was exhausted. So she used to scold and scold :

"You will have to tell all these people that you were lying, so that they don't all go around wasting their time on fairy tales and making me waste my time, as I can't get on with anything!"

And she would tell my father everything that had happened during the day, what they had said, the conclusions they had come to, etc. My father used to listen in silence, not knowing what to say, and before long he began to escape. When he arrived home at night to find the house full of people, he used to turn right round and go off until everybody had gone away.

This, too, upset my mother, and when my father went off like that she used to say:

"Why don't you stay and help me to get rid of the people?"

To which my father would reply:

"I simply do not know what to say to them and I'm fed up with all their questions."

The fact was that many people from round about used to call in to our house at night on the way home from work to find out what had been happening. They may well not have realised the trouble they were causing within our family circle.

34. The family property at Cova da Iria

My mother used to send my sisters to fetch basketfuls of greens and fruit from the Cova da Iria when they were needed. The crops from there were always good and fresh as my father used to cultivate them between the rows of maize or potatoes in the years in which he put the whole of the Cova da Iria under either maize or potatoes.

In other years, he used to sow either maize or potatoes in part of the property only, and keep the rest for growing vegetables – cabbages, turnips, string beans, onions, tomatoes, etc. – which all grew well there, because the Cova da Iria was irrigated by the water from a pool situated on the first ridge as you went up the slope, where the basilica now stands. The pool was situated more or less where the drinking fountain now is.

Thanks to some channels that my father had made for the purpose, the water from the pool used to run down the Cova, keeping it moist and fertile, in conjunction with the waters from the two slopes that brought down there the moisture from the leaves from the trees and the undergrowth when it rained.

There in the Cova, up against the earth supporting wall that marked off the first ridge as you went up, where the basilica now stands, there was an avenue of fruit trees, apples and pears, and perhaps others, I don't remember. Up against the low wall that separated our property from that of our neighbour, on the Fatima side, there were two orange trees and a lemon tree, which were also irrigated by the water from the pool that ran down there through a channel my father had made in the soil for that purpose.

Around the pool there was a lot of fresh hay and broom which was used to make sweeping brushes. The sheep used to drink in between the hay, in the little holes that the water from the pool hollowed out of the ground. We ourselves used to drink the water, too, drawing it out with a cabbage leaf in the form of a shell.

At the time, child that I was, I did not know how to assess the value of the produce from the land, nor did I bother my head about it. However, Dr José Galamba da Oliveira, who made a study of Fatima when everything was still as it was, and he was able to speak to the people living at the time, said on page 155 (8th edition) of his book *"Jacinta"* that the Cova used to yield 50 sacks of potatoes. In the years when part of the land was used for growing vegetables, the potato yield would have been less, depending on the size of the relative areas the different crops occupied. The same applies when the Cova was sown with maize instead of potatoes.

In addition, there was the yield from the olive, holm oak, chestnut and arbutus trees, etc., and, at the top, where the rear of the Basilica now is, there was a stretch of flat ground where my father used to cultivate vegetables, chick-peas and lupins and, in other years, wheat, rye, etc. Some years one, other years another, according to need.

35. The crops from the Cova are destroyed

To go back to what I was saying, namely that my mother used to send my sisters to the Cova to get baskets of vegetables and fruit for our own use in the house. One day my mother sent them and they went, but they came back with empty baskets, saying that there was nothing left in the Cova da Iria that could be used. Everything had been destroyed, trampled on by the people and by the animals. (Many of the people went there on horseback; then they used to turn their ass or horse loose to graze, with the result that they trampled on everything, eating, or nibbling at, everything, including the tips of the trees.) All that was left was some of the fruit, at the tips of the branches where no-one could reach.

My mother said :

"Heavens above! That's all I needed to have to cope with at the end of my life! And all on account of the nonsense these children have invented and gone spreading abroad. And no-one can get them to go back on what they have said, and admit that they lied. And there are people foolish enough to believe them and go running there and praying in front of a holm oak, whereas Our Lord is in the tabernacle in the Church and no-one goes there! And how are we going to manage without the produce from the Cova da Iria? God help me! Come on, child, make up your mind and admit that you lied, so that all this will come to an end and we can live in peace in our house once more."

I understood my mother's anguish, and the upheaval that the whole affair was creating in our house. At the same time, God knows how much I myself suffered! For, as my mother said, I was the cause of it all and if I would only say that I had lied, I could put an end to it all. But I thought: "If I say that I lied, then I will indeed be telling a lie, and that will make the Lady who comes to the Cova sad!" God alone knows what a fierce battle was being fought inside me, almost as if heaven and earth were at war.

36. At night, when the visitors had gone

At night when all the people had gone, my mother would get the supper ready and when we were all assembled in the kitchen, waiting for my father to come home for supper, she would look at all the empty places – my father's, who had not yet arrived, and my two sisters, who had been married. Being sad and distressed, and bemoaning the whole affair, she would bend over a little table that used to be in the kitchen, put her head in her hands and start sobbing, so much so that the rest of us began to cry with her. All this moved me deeply, all the more so since never before had I seen my mother cry. One day, my sister Gloria, who was beside me, started to shake me, saying:

"Can't you see? All this is your fault. Do what Mother asks, say that you lied and put an end to all these stories!"

I didn't know what to do. Not wanting to stay there and make my mother suffer even more, I got up, crying and praying, and went down to the well and bowed down over the stones that covered it, deeply distressed and asking myself :

"What shall I do? If I say that I lied in order to put an end to it all, then I shall be telling a lie. If I don't, my mother will die of sorrow, and it will be impossible to live in our house! To say that I saw nothing is to tell a lie, and to tell a lie is to offend God, and I don't want to offend God. I'd rather die and He can take me to Heaven".

All these thoughts kept going through my head, but when it seemed to me that I ought to do what my mother wanted by saying that I had lied and so put an end to the whole thing, I felt within me a superior strength which made it impossible for me to say a word.

In the meantime, my father arrived home and when he saw that I was not at supper, he came to look for me. He found me by the well and asked me what I was doing there. I told him that Mother was crying because of the Lady who had appeared in the Cova da Iria and that I did not know what to do. My father took my hand and said:

"Come on, let's go home and have our supper."

And so the two of us went back to the house. When we got there, the atmosphere was a little bit calmer. My mother told my father everything that had happened with the people during the day and how my sisters had been to fetch greens from the Cova da Iria but had brought back nothing as it had all been trampled on [because] the people came there on horseback and turned their horses and donkeys loose to graze, with the result that they had gnawed at, and trampled on, everything, even the tips of the trees; all that was left was some of the fruit, at the tips of the branches where no-one could reach. My father said that he would go and see as soon as he had the time. And he went, as I have already described in the Fifth Memoir.

37. More and more people

While the apparitions continued, more and more people kept coming to the Cova da Iria, and to our house, wanting to see me and speak to me. Some had faith and believed in the apparitions; others had none, and they were making fun and criticising, and saying it was all nonsense, etc. Some laid the blame on my parents, saying that they did not know how to educate their children, that if the children were theirs, they would have found a way to put an end to these stories of visions, etc. My mother did not answer these people. She listened in silence and when they had gone, she used to cry, not knowing what to make of life! It was at such times, when she was upset, that she redoubled her efforts to get me to admit that I had lied and put an end to it all so that we could once more live in peace. It was at such times that she sometimes went so far as to punish me by beating me. Not in anger, but like some-one who has a duty to educate, in the same way as it was the custom for teachers to use a ferule in the schools.

My mother was right; God alone knows how much she suf-fered, and He has surely rewarded her for it all in Heaven.

Some of the people who came were very importunate. They would listen to no apologies or excuses, and refused to leave the house until I came to speak to them.

My mother was distressed by it all and did not know what to do. My father and my two sisters Gloria and Carolina had to go out to work in the fields. My mother was alone in the house, and had no-one that she could send to call me. It needed to be someone who could go and call me, and then look after the sheep in my place, so that I could leave them. My mother could not go herself and leave all those people alone in our house. And if she were to ask a neighbour to go and call me and tell me to bring the sheep into the pen, where was she going to find food for so many animals for the rest of the day? Thus the difficulties with which my mother was faced increased day by day.

Quite often, almost every day in fact, with so many people in the house, she could not get on with her housework, and it was only at night when I returned with the sheep and was able to attend to the people and they finally went away that my mother could do the most necessary tasks and prepare the supper for the family.

38. My father's place of refuge

One day when my brother and my two sisters Gloria and Caro-lina, who had already returned from work in the evening, were do-ing the various household tasks and preparing the supper, my mother sent me to call my father to come home to supper. So I went to look for him. I went first to Godmother Teresa's wine cellar, where he usually was, playing cards with Godfather Anastácio and some others – this was after he began to find outsiders still in our house at night when he came home. If he wasn't there, I used to go and look for him in a tavern in Casa Velha – thank God there was no such plague of a place in Aljustrel – to which some false friends of his, taking advantage of the situation, had inveigled him to go so that they could play cards with him, something which my father enjoyed very much.

As I have already said elsewhere, my father used to spend the afternoon on Sundays and on Holidays of Obligation with my uncles and others playing cards in our yard. It was only later, when they could not go there to play because of all the people, that they began to play elsewhere. At that time it was the only form of entertainment for men. And it was to this that I referred in my other Memoirs when I said that my father, led on by false friends, had got hooked on a bad habit: it was to the card playing that I was referring. I then went on to say "this meant the loss of some of our property". [16] This was not correct, so let me explain: I was still only a child at the time and did not bother my head about what we had. I overheard my mother say that my father had become embroiled with false friends and that he was hooked on card playing. At the same time she was complaining about the loss of the land at Cova da Iria – the hollow itself [*cova* = hollow, in Portuguese], the slopes, the produce which was so badly needed in order to manage the household and feed the family. Because of all this, I was left with the impression that in playing cards, my father had lost some other property, but that was not so, thanks be to God! But it was only a long time later, when my sisters got to know what I had written, that they told me that this particular detail was incorrect and explained to me how our father had never either destroyed or lost any of our property. But what I had written had already been published and I did not know how to correct what I had said.

The stake my father played for was never anywhere near enough to ruin a family's property. Each one used to put a coin of a value agreed between the players, which would be 10 *réis or 1 vintém* or at most 1 *tostão*. The winner took all the coins but often only to lose them in the next game. The worst part was that all the time that they played, they had in front of them a jug of wine, and they used to drink a glassful at the end of each round. Neverthe-

---

[16] *Cf. 2nd Memoir, op. cit. p. 66*

less, I never knew my father to drink to the point of losing control of himself, or of coming home talking nonsense and disturbing the family peace, or maltreating people either verbally or physically. But this was the basis of the exaggerated things that people said about him.

39. My father: a prudent man

Whenever I went to call him to come home to supper, as soon as he saw me, he used to ask whether all the people had gone. When I told him that they had, he would get up at once and say farewell with the customary greeting: *até amanhã* (lit. : 'See you tomorrow'). Then he would take my hand and walk back home with me talking naturally. During supper, he would listen calmly to all that my mother had to say: her complaints about the people who came and who were sometimes so intrusive that she did not know how to deal with them or satisfy them, and the countless other difficulties that presented themselves, finishing up with:

"If only you would come home, you could help me to attend to these people and get rid of them, but, so far, you've got only yourself entangled with these false friends of yours and your passion for cards, and you don't put in an appearance. What a life! God help me!"

My father's calm response to all this was to say:

"You are right, but I don't come precisely in order not to have to encounter those people, because if I see them here in my house insulting the little one and being unkind to her, I might lose my patience and put them out in a way they wouldn't like. So I think it is better for me not to be here. And if it is Our Lady who is appearing there, She will help us!"

To which my mother would reply:

"Our Lady! What Our Lady? You persist in thinking that it is Our Lady. I only wish it were Our Lady, because then She would help us in some other way. But as it is, with all this upset and disturbance here in the house, with me being troubled and tormented and not knowing where to turn, it seems more like the devil who has got into the house with us! He has carried you off with those false friends and your passion for cards; and he has made life black for me here in the house. God help us!"

I think my mother was right in this, because wherever God is at work, the devil and his followers are sure to be there too, to see if they can somehow thwart God's work and, if possible, tear it up by the roots.

Today, I thank God that that was how it was. It is one more sign that the work was His. Had it not been, the devil with his followers would not have been so much up in arms, nor would they have fought so strenuously against it.

But I rest in God, because only God is great, only God is strong, wise and powerful, exceeds all things and triumphs!

Sometimes, my mother used to ask my father to see if he could persuade me to say that I had lied. And he would reply:

"Don't worry so much. We don't know that it is true, but we also don't know that it is not. Let us wait patiently until we see how the whole thing turns out."

And my mother would reply:

"How it turns out?! There is no sign of it coming to an end. More and more people coming from all over the place, and coming here, going to the Cova da Iria, with donkeys and horses and making it look like a procession of ants. There isn't even anything left for the animals to eat any more, it is all stones and nothing more!

I have never in my life seen anything like it! And we have the Church, with the Lord in the Blessed Sacrament, but instead of going there, they go to the Cova da Iria to pray in front of a holm oak. Did you ever hear of such madness? God help us. If this child were to make up her mind to say that she lied, it would be finished with once and for all. But no! No-one can get it out of her, obstinate as only she knows how to be. And what is more, she used not to be like that. God help us. I simply do not know what to do!"

Nor did I know what to do! But today, I thank God in the words of Psalm 22 :

The Lord is my shepherd; there is nothing I shall want.
Fresh and green are the pastures
where he gives me repose.
Near restful waters he leads me,to revive my drooping spirit.
He guides me along the right path; he is true to his name.
If I should walk in the valley of darkness
no evil would I fear.

You are there with your crook and your staff;
with these you give me comfort.
You have prepared a banquet for me in the sight of my foes.
My head you have anointed with oil; my cup is overflowing.
Surely goodness and kindness shall follow me
all the days of my life.
In the Lord's own house shall I dwell for ever and ever.

40. *"Perhaps they'll get her to admit that she lied"*

All these difficulties and afflictions bring us to the month of August and to the day on which the Administrator of Vila Nova de Ourém sent orders for my father to bring me to his office together with Uncle Marto with his two children, Francisco and Jacinta.

Uncle Marto said that he would go but he would not bring the children as they were very small and could not walk that far, neither could they go on horseback as they were not used to riding.

My father said :

"I'm taking my little one with me. I don't understand anything about these things, and I don't know what to say."

My mother actually seemed pleased, and said :

"Take her. Take her. They can't do any harm to a little one like that. And maybe, now, these Republicans, who don't want prayers or anything to do with God or with Our Lady, will get her to admit that she lied, and so we'll be done with this business once and for all."

The next day, she got up early, made breakfast for myself and for my father, harnessed the donkey for me to ride – my father was going to walk with Uncle Marto, who had no mount – and when it was time for us to go she put me sitting on the donkey, saying:

"Off you go now, and mind you don't fall." She then adjusted my father's tie and his waistband –which men wore in those days instead of a belt– saying:

"Here's hoping that you come back with this whole thing settled and that those Republicans will succeed in getting the little one to admit that she lied and so put an end to the whole affair once and for all. God go with you and so be it; see you later, please God."

And off we went, as I have already described in the other Memoirs. When we returned, my mother ran at once to ask my father how things had gone, and my father replied:

"They wanted the little one to tell them the secret, but she said that she could not reveal it. They reprimanded Marto for not bringing his children, and they sent us away. I have lost a day's work that I badly needed. Patience."

My mother said:

"Time wasted, and we with so much to do!"

That night, when we were all having our supper, my sister Maria came with her husband to ask Father what had happened and what the Administrator had wanted. My father repeated what he had already said to my mother:

"They wanted the little one to tell them the secret, but she said that she could not reveal it. They reprimanded Marto for not bringing his children, and they sent us away. I have lost a day's work that I badly needed. Patience!"

And my mother added:

"I was hoping that those Republicans would have forced the little one to say that she had been lying. But no! Things are as they were. God help us all!"

A few days later, on the morning of 13th August 1917, my father was again summoned to appear, with me, in Uncle Marto's house, where the Administrator was, and wanted to speak to me.

At first, my father did not want to go. He said that he had taken me to Vila Nova de Ourém only a few days before where the Administrator had both seen me and spoken to me.

"What more does he want?"

But when she heard this, my mother urged my father to go and to take me:

"Who knows," she said, "maybe this time, with Francisco and Jacinta as well, they will succeed in getting the children to say that they lied and bring this whole affair to an end. Go on, go there and see!"

Urged on by my mother, my father took me by the hand and, walking through quite a crowd of people who had come to meet us, took me to Uncle Marto's house, where the Administrator already was, asking Francisco and Jacinta questions.

I won't describe what happened on this occasion as I have already described the events in a number of places and they are well known. What I think it is important to describe here is my mother's attitude to what was happening.

So I shall describe what she did. As I have already said elsewhere, the Administrator came a second time when he brought us back to Fatima.

It must have been a Sunday or Holiday of Obligation because only on those days was the Church full of people at Mass, thus obeying the Church's commandment to hear Mass on Sundays and on Holidays of Obligation. On this particular day – which I think must have been 19th August [17] – the Church was full of people. When Mass was over, they all came out into the square. It was then that people realised that we were on the verandah of the parish priest's house with the Administrator, having arrived a few minutes earlier.

When they saw us, the people came running, wanting to climb up the steps leading to the presbytery verandah to get close to us and kiss us, but the Administrator signalled to them not to come up.

My father and Uncle Marto, however, did come up. My father took hold of my hand, went down the steps with me, and took me over to my mother who was at the bottom of the steps with my sisters. Aunt Olimpia and the others hugged me and we set off for Aljustrel with Aunt Olimpia, Jacinta and Francisco, who had come down the steps running behind me to get to their mother, while Uncle Marto remained behind talking to the Administrator.

On the way, we were showered with questions about what had happened to us, whether or not we had been maltreated. I said 'no', because to me the word 'maltreat' suggested being beaten, and we hadn't been beaten.

People were bidding each other goodbye in the ordinary way, while others kept on walking along the road to Casa Velha, Eira da Pedra, Pederneira, etc.

When we got to our house, we said goodbye to the people. The first thing my mother did was to wash me, comb my hair and put clean clothes on me, while my sisters, Gloria and Carolina, got the meal ready. My father and my brother saw to the animals. Then I sat down to dinner with all the family. While we were eating, there

---

[17] *The seers returned to Fatima from Vila Nova de Ourém on 15th August, feast of the Assumption of Our Lady. Cf. DCF-1. doc. 40. p. 296, note 20, and doc. 31, p. 262.*

was only one topic of conversation: questions about what had happened, where we had been taken, what they had done to us, what they had said to us, had they given us anything to eat, what had they wanted. I said that they wanted us to reveal to them the secret, but that as this could not be, they had brought us back to Fatima.

My father said:

"Maybe they are afraid that it is all a Royalist trick to stir up a rebellion and restore the monarchy."

My mother replied:

"That could be what they are thinking and so they are afraid, and it wouldn't be a bad idea. Since they came to power prices have gone up so much! The tithes and taxes are so high that the people hardly earn enough to pay them, and then there is war and more war taking the young men away to die on their behalf. If only they would leave us in peace to live our Christian lives. But no! They go around preaching new doctrines to deceive the people. God help us with such people!"

News of our return to Fatima spread rapidly, and soon people began arriving asking to see me and to speak to me. They were all asking the same questions: what had they done to us; where had they taken us; what did they want, and so on. And I gave the same replies. Seeing this, my mother said it would be better for me to go with our sheep to Valinhos, which was nearby, and anyone who wanted to speak to me could go there with me.

Aunt Olimpia said she would not let either Francisco or Jacinta go with the sheep as she had not yet had time to wash them, comb their hair and dress them, so she sent John with me, with their sheep.

I have already described elsewhere everything else that happened that day, including the apparition in Valinhos, [18] so I won't repeat it here, except to add clarification of some of the details which, due to lack of time and opportunity, I did not explain very clearly, in the belief that – in order to keep my account short – I only needed to recount the bare facts without going into the details of

---

[18] *The apparition in Valinhos took place on August 19th "the Sunday after August 13th". Cf. DCF-1, doc. 4, p. 17; doc. 31, p. 260 and 262.*

circumstances, times and places. As a result some wrong impressions were created and questions were asked by people who thought they saw a contradiction between what I said then and what I am saying now.

41. Clarifications

I wrote the Memoirs out of obedience to the Bishop of Leiria, D. José Alves Correia da Silva, who asked me, indeed, ordered me to do so. However, I wrote them in the midst of many difficulties, lack of the necessary time and opportunity in which to write something that would be approved of, and recognising at the same time that I did not have the necessary education, which made me think that the manuscript would be no use, and would not be used.

This enabled me to write freely as the various events came back to my mind, without being concerned about order, times, places, and without the time or opportunity to read over and correct what I had written. Thus it was that some details were not sufficiently explained as to the time and place where they occurred. So that is what I am going to do now, so that they will be better understood.

In the second Memoir, I wrote: "at the end of my three years as a shepherdess, from the time I was seven until I was ten years old".[19] I should have written: "During my four years as a shepherdess, from the time I was seven until I was twelve." This is because I then described incidents that took place when I was between 7 and 12 years old. I should have said: "During these five years."

I wrote: "During this period... my father had fallen into bad company and let his weakness get the better of him".[20] I was referring to his card playing. This happened during the period of the apparitions.

I wrote: "this meant the loss of some of our property".[21] This was due to a misunderstanding on my part. I had heard my mother say so often what a loss the produce from the Cova da Iria, both

---

[19] Cf. *Second Memoir, 11th English ed., p. 65.*
[20] Cf. *Second Memoir, 11th ed., p. 66.*
[21] Cf. *Second Memoir, 11th ed., p. 66.*

the slopes and the hollow, was to us, and at the same time I had heard her lamenting the fact that my father did not come straight home from work as he used to do. This left me with the impression that my father had lost some of the rest of our property at cards. This was the weakness to which I was referring, but in fact this he did not lose anything.

When my sisters came to know what I had written, they explained this point to me and told me that our father had never either played for, or sold, any of our lands, and that my mother was only speaking of the Cova da Iria, with its slopes and hollow. Card playing was the only distraction and entertainment available for men at that time, and the stakes they played for were not enough to ruin a family. Each player used to place in the middle of the table a coin the value of which would have been agreed between the players: perhaps 10 *réis* or 1 *vintém* or at most 1 *tostão*. The winner took all the coins, but he had to treat all the players to a glass of wine. Thus, each one lost a little and gained a little.

I wrote: "When my mother realised that our means of livelihood were diminishing, she resolved to send my two sisters, Gloria and Carolina, out to work as servants. At home there remained only my brother, to look after our few remaining fields (I meant by this : in addition to the Cova da Iria); my mother to take care of the house; and myself to take our sheep out to pasture". [22] This was during the apparitions, when we were left without the Cova da Iria, its slopes and the hollow, which were very much needed to feed the family.

I wrote: "My poor mother seemed just drowned in the depths of distress. When we gathered round the fire at night time, waiting for my father to come in to supper, my mother would look at her daughters' empty places and exclaim with profound sadness :

"My God, where has all the joy of our home gone?"

Then, resting her head on a little table beside her, she would burst into bitter tears [23].

This happened during the period of the apparitions, until one day it occurred to my mother, when she had finally got rid of all the people and was busy getting the supper while my brother attended

---

[22]   *Cf. Second Memoir, 10th English edition, p. 66.*
[23]   *Cf. Second Memoir, 10th English edition, p. 66.*

to the animals, giving them the last feed of the day, to send me to call my father to come to supper. So I went and as soon as he saw me, he used to ask whether all the people had gone. When I told him they had, he used to get up and say goodbye [to his friends] and, taking my hand, walk back home with me quite happily. As he took his supper with all the family, he would listen to whatever I had to say, and to the problems my mother told him about, and at the end, would say grace as usual. If there was husking or other similar work to be done on the threshing floor, such as winnowing the corn, maize, wheat, rye, etc. to be stored during the year, or if there were broad beans, string beans, peas, etc. to be de-podded and the seeds kept for the coming year, he always did his share, directing the work while at the same time happily enjoying the fresh air that blew there, by the light of the moon and of the lamps that used to be hung on the posts that stood round the threshing floor. Then, when the time came, he would declare the work at an end for the day and go to bed with the rest of the family.

Neither I nor my sisters (whom I asked about this) ever heard anyone say that my father had drunk too much, to the point of losing control of himself, or of coming home talking nonsense and maltreating people, either in word or deed, or of disturbing the peace and tranquillity of the family environment. But it was of all this that people were thinking when they said exaggerated things about him.

42. My father: a peaceable man

À propos of all this, I shall now relate what happened one day, during the period of the apparitions, though I don't remember on what day or in which month. At the time I did not know how to read or write and I attached no importance to dates.

It was what I now call the beginning of the diabolical struggle against the Message, although it may well be that my parents did not realise this, nor I myself, at the time. Today, however, I seem to see it all very clearly, without a shadow of doubt.

We were all assembled in the house for supper. Someone called from outside; I went to see who it was. It was my father's false friends who wanted to have a word with him. My father overheard and came out to see what they wanted. My mother came too, and they both stood close to the door of the kitchen. The men began to say to my father that, in view of what had happened that afternoon at the Cova da Iria, he ought bring an action against the man who had maltreated him on his own property, where the man had no right to be, and "all because you had ordered the people who were there to get out because they had already caused a lot of damage, destroying your entire crop for this year." They assured him that he would win his case as the civilian government and even the Administrator would be on his side, because this was just what they all wanted: to have done with this affair. They would even force the man who had attacked him, and the people who were trespassing on his property, to pay for all the damage they had caused, and so on.

My father listened to them in silence and then said:

"No, I am not going to do this. I prefer to forgive them so that God may forgive me my sins too; all I want is to live in peace and harmony with everybody."

My mother, who was standing beside my father, then said:

"How could you bring an action against all the people who go there every day? It's so and so today, so and so else tomorrow; none of the local people know them or where they come from. And this endless procession of people coming here from all over the place, without anyone knowing who they are, or where they come from, or where they are going to! Look, I am going ask you to do something for me. Please don't keep coming after my husband, trying to lead him astray and into bad ways!"

With that, she pulled my father back into the house and slammed the door shut, saying :

"What a lot! It's almost as if the devil was with them!"

We sat down to our supper, and my mother asked my father what had happened that afternoon in the Cova da Iria that they should come looking for him with such a proposal.

My father replied:

"They came to look for me, and said that I should go to the Cova da Iria and order all those people off [the property] as they had already done a lot of damage to this year's crops. I went, but as soon as I got there and told the people to go, one of them rushed at me so forcefully when I was not expecting it that he knocked me down. When I got up and saw that I could do nothing in the face of so many people, I withdrew."

My mother replied :

"Hmm, and now they want you to bring a lawsuit. Whatever for? So that we'll have to pay fees to a lawyer on top of everything else. You can do nothing in the face of so many people."

There was a man in Aljustrel who had brought a lawsuit against a neighbour. This man came to my father to ask him to be a witness on his behalf, but my father said:

"Please don't come asking me to do this, because, in these matters, I believe it is best for people to forgive so that God will forgive us our sins too and we can live in peace and tranquillity with all, even if we do lose something in the process."

As I write this, I am reminded of the story of Abraham and his nephew Lot: «Let there be no strife between you and me, and between your herdsmen and my herdsmen, for we are kinsmen.. Take your choice.... If you take the right hand, then I will go to the left; if you take the left hand, then I will go to the right.» [Cf. Genesis, 13, 8-10].

If all men were like that, there would not be so many wars in the world, nor so many disputes in families, nor such discord between brothers! And why? Often it is all on account of a little bit of pride, or covetousness, or a desire for revenge, or over a little bit of land that no-one can take in the coffin with them when God calls them into his presence to give an account of everything to the One from whom nothing is hidden, nothing escapes or goes unnoticed, and before Whom the only accuser is one's own conscience which, there, can deny nothing and makes one conscious of one's own unworthiness. Great is the mercy of God towards all. And He forgives all if, before we leave this world, we repent, ask pardon and ourselves grant pardon, and do penance.

«Blessed are the peace-makers, for they shall be called the children of God» (Mt. 5,9).

Thus, I believe that God in his mercy has received my father into his Kingdom as one of his children. This faith and confidence fill me with peace and joy, with the hope of one day finding myself in the Kingdom of Heaven in the company of those whom God chose to give me the gift of life. Poor they may have been in this world's goods, but that doesn't matter, because earthly things pass away. Heaven abides for ever!

43. My mother's incredulity

I have already said in the other Memoirs, and don't want to repeat it here, that my mother did not believe that the apparitions really had happened. It seemed to her incredible that Our Lady should come down from Heaven in order to speak to three poor children.

After the episode of three of us having been taken off to prison, people asked my mother had she not been worried, wondering what might be happening to the three children. But she replied:

"No, I wasn't worried. I thought to myself: if they really did see Our Lady, she will take care of them; but if they are telling lies, it is only right that they should be forced to tell the truth. Those people won't do any great harm to three such little children, and since the Republicans want to have nothing to do with God or Our Lady, perhaps they will succeed in forcing them to admit that they lied, and put an end to this affair once and for all. God grant it may be so!"

When the Administrator brought us back to Fatima, and the apparition in Valinhos took place, my mother said:

"If that Lady is going to begin appearing in Valinhos, so much the better. Maybe then the people will come here and stop going to the Cova da Iria. Here in Valinhos they won't cause so much damage because the ground is not under crops." But when she heard us say that the Lady had told us to continue going to the Cova da Iria, she said :

"Heavens above, things are just the same. Not even the Republicans were able to put an end to all this."

One of the people who came to our house to ask what had happened during the days that the Administrator had kept the three little shepherds in custody, what he wanted with them, whether he had maltreated them, etc. was a little man from Casais.

My mother said: "They say they were not maltreated."

We said that we had not been maltreated because to us 'maltreat' meant being beaten and we hadn't been beaten...

"I was hoping [my mother went on] that they would have forced them to confess and admit that they had lied and so undeceive all these people and bring the whole affair to an end. But not a bit of it! Things are the same as ever!"

The little man replied :

"But look here, 'Aunt' Maria Rosa. How could you expect the Republicans to force the little shepherds to make a confession and say that they had lied, when they themselves do not go to confession? They want nothing to do with priests or friars or Sisters – they are the very people who have just put them all out of the country; they have closed the churches and forbidden us to ring the bells or to hold processions; they rob everything that belongs to the Church. Look at our own little church, which had a few little olive trees from which we got enough oil to keep the Blessed Sacrament lamp alight: they have seized everything. They say it belongs to them, and that's that! Now it's we who have to give the oil to keep the lamp lit. But that is not the worst of it. The worst of it is that they have got involved in wars and they are sending our boys out to die, pierced through with cannon balls. Who knows, 'Aunt' Maria Rosa, maybe Our Lady will come and save us?"

My mother replied :

"Our Lady! If only it were Our Lady. But not a bit of it! Here in my own house I no longer have any peace or rest with all these people coming and knocking on my door, so that I can get nothing done. And I have so much to do. And then there's the problem of the little one. They want to see her, and she goes out with the sheep and I have no-one to send and call her who can stay and look after the sheep in her place! I am tormented, and I simply do not know where to turn. God help me!"

44. Hard times

More and more people kept coming and knocking at our door asking to see and to speak to me, and this was a true martyrdom for my mother. My father, with my brother and my two sisters, Gloria and Carolina, used to go out early in the morning to work in the fields. And I went off with the sheep, leaving my mother alone in the house. The people who came were reluctant to go away again without having seen me and spoken to me. My mother had no-one to send and call me and remain in my place to keep an eye on the sheep. And if she were to send and tell me to bring the sheep back to the fold, where would she find enough to feed so many animals for the rest of the day? It was a difficult problem, and she did not know how to solve it. In the end she resolved to discuss the matter with my father, who said he thought it would be best to sell the sheep and send me to school. Then the people who came looking for me could be told to go and ask for me at the school. Thus, even though we would feel acutely the loss of everything that we derived from the flock, my parents decided to sell the sheep as they could find no other solution.

The loss we were already experiencing of the produce from the Cova da Iria, coupled with the loss of the yield from the sheep, meant that we were reduced to "our daily bread from day to day". We no longer had any curdled milk to drink with pieces of bread soaked in it at breakfast and at supper, or to make cheese with. [We also did not have the milk] to give in exchange for the goat's milk which we used to drink in the middle of the morning, for the afternoon snack, and at bedtime; nor did we have the young lambs which used to triple the size of the flock each year, as nearly all the ewes produced two lambs. Thus, in the spring, the flock would increase in number from the normal 30 to about 80 sheep in all. My father used to kill some of the lambs to feed the family. The remainder were sold, together with the ewe lambs that were not needed to replace the ewes in the flock that were old and worn out. These, too, were sold, and the money helped increase the family's finances. Moreover, we no longer had the wool that came from the sheep every year which was used to make warm clothing for the winter. Adding all this to the loss of the produce from the Cova da Iria, it was naturally my mother, who was responsible for the running of the house, who felt most the reduction in the family income and who worried most about it.

As a result, we were reduced to living from the produce of the other pieces of land that my parents possessed, which were smaller and less productive. Only hard and toilsome labour made it possible to extract from them enough to live on.

45. Confidence in God and sharing

In spite of our reduced circumstances, my mother said resignedly:

"I don't know what things will come to if we go on at this rate. But let's trust in God who has always helped us, and in the protection of Our Lady, who is my baptismal Godmother."

Moreover, in spite of everything, my mother never stopped helping the poor. She used to say: "We ourselves have little, but this little will have to stretch to help those who have less even than we have."

Thus she used to do as God said in the Bible: "You shall eat your bread by the sweat of your brow, and you shall help the poor in their need."

46. Poor, humble way of life

Dr José Galamba de Oliveira, who investigated the whole question of Fatima when things were still as they had been before the apparitions, and during the lifetime of all those involved, wrote in his book *Jacinta* (8th edition, p. 154): "The seers' families did not make a single *real* out of it all. They had been comfortably off. Jacinta's parents continued to be so. Lucia's family became impoverished."

In the pastoral letter that the Bishop of Leiria, Don José Alves Correia da Silva, wrote about devotion to Our Lady of Fatima in 1930, he had this to say about the seers' families: «There is no sign in them of any self-interest or vanity. They do not accept either the money or the gifts that people try to give them. And, when we decided to take over direction of the works and of the religious movement, they dutifully handed over intact the money and objects of value that the people, in their fervour, used to leave at the place of the apparitions. The children's parents were comfortably off and today they continue to live modestly. They lived by their work and they continue to live by their work. Nothing has changed in their lives over the past 13 years» (*1930 Pastoral Letter*).

Dr. José Galamba de Oliveira, too, had this to say about my parents: «The apparitions caused them a series of problems and difficulties» (*Jacinta,* p. 154). I should explain that Francisco and Jacinta's parents did not suffer in the same way, as Our Lady did not appear in any of the properties belonging to them.

And as for looking after the sheep, they had John, who was still small and whose task it was according to his age – he was 11 years old – to take the sheep to pasture at that time. Only it was not he who went, because Francisco and Jacinta had begged their parents to let them do it in order to be with me. Hence, my uncle and aunt did not experience our difficulties; they could send John to mind the sheep and keep Francisco and Jacinta at home. But they, too, sold their flock when they got ill with the flu.

But all this is part of God's plan, who chooses each one to accomplish the mission assigned to him or her. Thus, Christ says in the gospel «You did not choose me, but I chose you and appointed you that you should go and bear fruit and that your fruit should abide» (John 15, 16).

This choice calls for a corresponding fidelity as the Lord said elsewhere: «If any one would come after me, let them deny themselves, take up their cross and follow me» (Mt. 16, 24).

Every saving work of God rests on the pedestal of the redeeming Cross of Christ.

47. 13th October: doubts persist

And so we come to the day of 13th October 1917. There was a rumour that someone would throw a bomb at the time of the apparition and that everyone who was there would be killed. So my parents said:

"We'll go with her. If she is going to die, we want to die beside her."

And although the rain was pouring down when it was time to go, towards the middle of the morning, they left the house with me and attempted to thread their way through the crowd. After that, I lost sight of my mother. My father managed to lead me by the hand as far as the place of the apparitions. I did not see him again after that until that night when I was back in our house with them both.

In the days that followed, people asked my mother:

"Well, 'Aunt' Maria Rosa, now do you believe that Our Lady appeared in your Cova da Iria?"

To which my mother replied:

"I'm not quite sure. That it should actually be Our Lady is something so great that we are not worthy of it."

It probably never occurred to my mother to think that it is in our unworthiness that the greatness of God's mercy manifests itself. As Our Lady herself said in her wonderful canticle, the Magnificat :

«The Lord has looked down on the lowliness of his handmaid. All generations will call me blessed.» (Luke 1, 48).

On other occasions, people came along to congratulate her on the fact that Our Lady had appeared to one of her children.

My mother's response to this was:

"I still don't know whether this is all true."

"But didn't you see the miracle of the sun?" they asked.

"Yes, I saw it, but it seemed to me something so great that we are not worthy of it. So I am still asking myself if this can be true. And I don't know".

What made her think like that was her recognition of her own unworthiness and of the unworthiness of everyone in the family, together with her deep humility, which was such that she could well have said, in the words of St Peter: «Depart from us, Lord, for we are sinners!»

48. I am dying with you stuck in my heart!"

As a result of all the extra work, difficulties, upsets and doubts, my mother began to be ill. She consulted various doctors who came to the area. They all prescribed medicines, but these did her no good. She went to Leiria to consult a doctor there, but to no avail. She then went to see a doctor in Reguengo do Fetal, Dr Carvalho, who used to come and see people in São Mamede. He diagnosed a displaced kidney and [a problem] with one of the vertebrae in her spine. Among other remedies, he prescribed hot needle treatment in her spine. She got some relief from this treatment, but she had to go to São Mamede for it, and at that time there was no means of transport. One had to go either on foot or on horseback. If she went on horseback, the thudding of the horse's hooves caused her acute pain. If she went on foot, the distance was too much for her in her poor state of health. As she went, she used to sit down on a convenient boulder to rest for a while, and eventually arrived home dead tired from the walk and hardly able to breathe.

In the end she had to give up that treatment, with the result that she got worse until a day came when it seemed that her days on earth were numbered. The doctor was called, but he could do nothing for her. Then the parish priest was called to administer the last Sacraments, and the whole family assembled to embrace her for the last time and receive her last blessing, kissing her trembling dying hand. She began with my older sisters. Being the youngest, I was last. When my poor mother saw me, she raised herself up a little, hugged me tight and said:

"My poor little girl! What will become of you without your mother? I am dying with you stuck in my heart."

Then bursting into tears and sobbing bitterly, she clasped me more and more tightly in her arms and would not let me go.

My sister Maria pulled me forcibly away from her, took me out to the kitchen, and forbade me to go back into my mother's room, saying:

"Our mother is dying of sorrow because of you and all the trouble you have caused."

I knelt down and put my head on a bench and with a deep sadness the like of which I had never felt in my life before, I offered my sacrifice to God, and begged that my mother would recover. Shortly afterwards, my two sisters, Maria and Teresa came up to me and said:

"Lucia, if you really did see Our Lady, go now to the Cova da Iria and ask her to heal our mother. Make her whatever promise you like; we will fulfil it. And then we will believe."

I got up and set off. In order to avoid meeting people, I went by some short cuts across the fields on the moor side, praying the Rosary as I went. I finished it on my knees bowed down over the place of the holm oak where Our Lady had appeared. I was in floods of tears as I presented my request to Our Lady, asking her to heal my mother and promising at the same time to go there on nine successive days with my sisters to say the Rosary on our knees as we made our way from the road to the place where the holm oak had been on which She had appeared; and on the last day to bring nine poor children with me and afterwards give them a meal.

49. "I already feel better, thank God"

Buoyed up with the hope that Our Lady would grant me this grace, I then got up and went home. When I got there, I found my sister Gloria in the kitchen and she said to me:

"Lucia, come here. Mother is already better."

As soon as my father, who was sitting with my mother in the bedroom, heard us talking, he came to meet me, took me by the hand and said:

"Come and give your mother a kiss. She is much better."

My mother was sitting up in bed sipping a bowl of chicken broth. My father took it from her and held it so that she could kiss me.

"Where did you go to, little one? Did you go and ask Our Lady to heal me?" my mother asked.

"Yes, I did," I replied.

"I already feel better, thanks be to God."

My father then gave the bowl back to my mother for her to finish the broth, and he sat down on a little chest they had in their room near the head of the bed. Then he took me on his knees and asked me where I had been and what I had done. I told him that I had been to the Cova de Iria to say the Rosary, and to ask Our Lady to heal Mother, promising to go there with my sisters for nine days in succession to say the Rosary and to go on our knees from the road to the place itself and, on the last day, to bring nine poor children with me, and afterwards give them a meal.

My father said:

"As soon as your mother is well and has got her strength back, we will all go and we will do it all in order to thank Our Lady for so great a grace."

Meanwhile my sister Gloria came with a bowl of broth and said:

"Take this, Lucia, as you probably haven't yet had anything to eat."

I said:

"No, not the broth; keep that for mother. I'll have something else."

But she insisted, saying:

"Go on, take it, as there's plenty for Mother. I am going to kill two more chickens for supper in order to make enough broth for everyone. Godmother Teresa is bringing everything else. She was here earlier on and said that she had everything ready to make supper for us and that she was gong to bring it, thinking that mother was dying. She is better, thank God, but Godmother Teresa is bringing everything just the same, and she and Godfather are coming here to have supper with us all. Maria and Teresa have gone back home for the moment but they, too, will be coming with their husbands to have supper with us."

Then both my mother and my father said that I should take the broth, so I took it.

50. *Supper and thanksgiving*

That night we had our supper in the front room with the door open so that everybody could see my mother. She wanted to get up, but my father would not let her, saying that she was very weak. She took her supper sitting up in bed, smiling at everyone, as she sipped another bowl of broth and then ate a little bit of chicken and rice.

The food for everyone to eat was placed on top of a large chest that stood in the front room, covered with a coarse home-spun linen cloth. The whole family was there: Godmother Teresa and Godfather Anastácio, actually in my mother's room, near the head of the bed; my father was seated on a small chest; I was sitting on a low stool next to him and then Godmother Teresa with her back to the window. The others were all in the outer room, some sitting on stools, others on chairs, others standing, holding their plates in their hands, everyone serving themselves and en-joying the food with healthy appetites. One by one, they came in turn into the bedroom to say their little piece, to which my mother replied with a smile, cheerful and happy to see them all there, all so happy together, as if she had been a hen with all her chickens round her, pecking at the ground and flying from one place to an-other, and all praising God: "Thanks be to God that Mother is so much better."

At the end of the meal, when my sisters had cleared every-thing away and washed up the dishes, my father said the usual grace after meals. Then my mother, sitting up in bed, started the Rosary in which everyone joined, kneeling, thanking God with her for the recovery Our Lady had obtained for her. At the end of the Litany, my mother, in thanksgiving, began to sing a hymn in which everyone joined:

> We seek God; ungrateful men
> The Almighty Father, the Redeemer,
> They lack faith, foolish men,
> They rise in vain against the Lord.

Bless, we pray, O holy Virgin,
Our cry of faith.
We seek God, who is our King,
We seek God who is our Father.

My father then told everyone the promise I had made when I was asking Our Lady to heal our mother. Everyone responded by saying:

"We'll go too." And they all went, as soon as my mother felt well enough for it. She herself wanted to go on her knees from the roadside to the place of the apparition, but my father would not let her. So she walked behind everyone, giving out the Rosary and keeping an eye on the poor children we had brought with us. We concluded the Rosary in the very place of the apparition. After the Litany, my mother intoned the hymn to Our Lady Patroness of Portugal :

Hail, noble Patron
Of your chosen people,
Chosen from among all
To be the people of the Lord.

Oh glory of our land,
Which you have rescued a thousand times,
As long as the Portuguese exist
You will be their loved one.

Your glory is to help us
You have no greater joy:
No-one calls on the name of Mary
And is left unaided.

You are our Patroness
You will not hand over to another
The care of the flock
Committed to your care.

You are the most sublime work of art
To issue from the hands of God!
Neither earth nor heaven
Contains a more perfect creature!

Afterwards, we returned home with the poor children and some of their mothers who had wanted to accompany us and unite their prayers with ours in thanksgiving to God and Our Lady.

The night before, my mother, with my sisters, had left everything for the meal ready in the large roasting pans in the oven.

My father, too, had left the sides of the ox cart in the yard to serve as a table; these were covered with cloths made of coarse homespun linen. So, when we got home, all we had to do was to go and get the large roasting pans and place them on the tables together with all the other things there were to eat, as well as the things my Godmother Teresa brought from her house (sweet rice and fruit) helped by Godfather Anastácio, who wanted to be the one to bring and provide the wine after they, too, had accompanied us to the Cova da Iria, praying and singing with us, and giving thanks to God and Our Lady.

We all sat down to eat together with the children and those of their mothers who had accompanied us.

There was enough for everyone, and my mother shared out what was left over between the various children, putting the meat into large loaves which she had baked for the purpose the evening before, in order to give one to each of them to take home with them; she placed these loaves with their fillings into stiff grey paper bags of the kind that were used at that time for such purposes. And so we all parted company, everyone happy and content, in thanksgiving to God and Our Lady.

From the third day of her recovery onwards, my mother continued her normal life for many years, though from time to time she did have a certain amount of discomfort, but nothing that prevented her from carrying out her ordinary household tasks.

"51. There's no way out of this!"

The year 1918 was the year of the flu epidemic. I have already described how my parents sacrificed themselves, going from door to door in order to take care of those who were ill, so I won't repeat it here.

My mother's biggest cross, at that time, was the continuous flow of people coming to see me and to speak to me.

By this time, I was going to school, which eased the situation a bit for my mother, as she used to send those who came [knocking at the door] to the school to look for me, but she saw how extremely tired and delicate I had become.

Some people, including Dr Formigão, warned her that I might be ill if she did not put a stop to so many visitors and questions. My mother saw what was happening, but what was she to do since those who were saying these things were the very people who came most often and asked the most wearisome, detailed and tiring questions. Each one of them wanted the others sent away but not they themselves, because they were well-intentioned and were somehow special!

My mother said :

"There is no way out of this. They all want me to send the rest away, but to let them come in. So what am I to do? How am I going to persuade the people who come to accept being sent away without having seen and spoken to the little one? They come into the house and refuse to go until she appears! It is easy to say, but not easy to do. God help me, I simply do not know where to turn!"

52. "Man, let her go, she'll be all right."

One day, Dr Carlos Mendes from Torres Novas came to ask my mother if she would allow him to take me to his house, so that he could educate me, and I would be able to study there. My mother agreed to this, subject to my father's agreement. They went to call him. My father said that if it were for a few days, so that I could have a rest, then he would allow me to go, but if the idea was that I should remain there always, then the answer was 'no'.

Dr Carlos Mendes used all the arguments suggested to him by his knowledge and skill as a lawyer in an effort to persuade my father to change his mind, but he did not succeed. My mother, too, tried to persuade him, saying:

"Let her go, man, she'll be alright. The Doctor is absolutely trustworthy and who knows, if she goes away from here, we'll have done with this whole affair!"

My father listened in silence to all the arguments and reasoning presented to him, but he would not give way.

Nevertheless, Dr Carlos Mendes did take me away with him for a few days, as my father had said he could – the Doctor may well have been hoping that when my father saw that I really was all right he would give way, but he didn't.

During my stay in the Doctor's house, I rested, and recovered quite a bit of my strength. Some people who got to know that I was there asked Dr Carlos Mendes if I could go to visit them in their houses, and he agreed to this. One of the people who did this was a Senhor Abel, who had a wife and one son, a little younger than myself. They had a shop on the ground floor, and the family lived upstairs.

Another was a Senhor Gilberto, who was the person who arranged for the statue of Our Lady of Fatima to be made, the one that is now venerated in the Chapel of the Apparitions. He lived with his parents, and was unmarried. He had a sister who was married to an Army officer. She, too, wanted to take me to her house, and I did go there for a short time, just to give her this pleasure.

I went to Mass and Communion every day with Dr Carlos Mendes and his wife, in the parish church of the town where he lived.

53. "Little houses, trotting along one behind the other."

One day, Dr Carlos and his wife took me for a walk behind the town. We were going to a property which I presume belonged to him. On the way, we passed close to the railway line and I saw a train for the first time. When, later on, I returned to Aljustrel, I described for the children who used to come and play with me in our front yard the great novelty that I had seen: a whole lot of little houses, trotting along one behind the other, without either horses or donkeys to pull them, and with lots of people inside and looking out the windows, and a great chimney in the front belching out smoke and hooting like a whole lot of horns sounding at once.

My mother was working nearby and overheard the conversation, so she came up to me and reprimanded me, saying :

"What's that you are saying? All we needed was for you to invent yet another story. Where did you see houses on wheels? What are you thinking of? Don't let me hear you saying such things again!"

I held my peace until much later on, when I went with my mother to Lisbon. When we were at the station waiting for the train, I made my way to the front to look down the track and see it as it approached. As soon as I spotted the train coming, I pulled my mother by the arm and said to her :

"Come here and look. Look! Can't you see the chimney whistling and belching out smoke, and the little houses trotting along one behind the other, and all the people inside?"

My mother said :

"You're right. I had never seen such a thing. What you said was true."

54. A few days in Reixida and Leiria

Another day, a lady from Reixida [24] asked for me to be allowed to spend a few days in her house. My mother said "yes" because it meant I could rest and be away from all the people and their questions who would not leave me in peace or give me a break.

So I went with Jacinta, and we spent a few quiet days there. At night we used to go with this lady and her family to say the Rosary in a little chapel close to her house. A lot of people from round about used to come too, filling the tiny chapel to overflowing. Everybody prayed with faith and devotion. One day, the lady took us to the Cortes, the home of a family who, I think, may have been related to her. There we met the local parish priest, who asked us a few questions. [25] We then returned to Aljustrel, a little bit refreshed from our weariness.

But the queues of people coming and going around me continued, and I again began to feel tired and exhausted. My mother was concerned and did not know what to do about it until one day it occurred to her to send me for a while to Leiria to stay with her brother, who was a policeman, and his wife and daughter. [26] My father agreed to this and he himself took me to Leiria.

---

[24] Maria do Carmo Marques da Cruz Meneses had the two little seers to stay with her in her house in Reixida, Cortes, Leiria, for eight days beginning on 14th or 15th September 1917.

[25] Fr António dos Santos Alves questioned the visionaries twice (Cf. DCF-I, doc. 44 and 45, p. 315-323).

[26] Manuel Ferreira Rosa, Maria José and Laura Varela (cf. Sixth Memoir, p. 52)

My uncle and aunt received me with the greatest joy and satisfaction. They treated me with the greatest delicacy, as if I had been their own daughter. My aunt used to bring me my breakfast in bed in the morning and insisted that I should rest until the middle of the morning. In the afternoons, the two little Varela girls, who were my aunt and uncle's nieces (their father was the brother of my aunt who had married my mother's brother), used to come and take me over to their house – they lived a little further up the road, on the opposite side – in order to play with them, as their house was more suitable for playing in, as they had a little garden at the back. There were three sisters and a brother. The brother was away studying, somewhere abroad, I think, but I'm not absolutely sure. The oldest girl was already grown up and was engaged to marry a young man from Lisbon, where she later went to live. The other two were younger, the youngest being a little older than myself.

In front of their house there was a road which wound its way up a little hill nearby. From time to time, the little girls' mother and my aunt used to prepare an afternoon snack for everyone in both families. Then we would all go there in the afternoon where there was a fresh breeze, almost like the Serra d'Aire. Sr. Varela and my uncle used to go to a kiosk nearby and buy fizzy drinks for us all to take with our snack.

On other days, and especially on Sundays, we used to go for our afternoon snack to the Hill of Our Lady of the Incarnation, which overlooked the back of my uncle and aunt's house. We used to eat our snack sitting on a flight of stone steps that stood there, shortly before you came to the chapel, where we went afterwards to say the five mysteries of the Rosary before the lovely image of Our Lady. After that, we used to go down the hill singing religious hymns and regional songs, accompanied by a guitar that my uncle played well. When we reached the road at the bottom of the hill, the people who lived there used to come out of their houses or look out of the windows and clap their hands and wave with their hands or with handkerchiefs, to show that they had enjoyed listening to us. I'm not sure, but I don't think they knew who the group of people were who were passing by.

In fact, I don't think many people realised that I was there. Only three families, who were friends of my aunt and uncle, and customers of my cousin Laura, who was a dressmaker, asked if I could visit their homes. My aunt and uncle said I could go and so I went.

The first was the Patrício family. They lived in a tall house, on the road leading to the Cathedral, on the left-hand side, with a shoe shop on the ground floor. One entered the building at the back, climbing up a bit of a slope. A lady, Dona Amélia, lived on the first floor with her brother who, like her, was unmarried, though he was engaged to be married to a girl from Lisbon, I think; they had two servants. A sister of theirs, Elvira, lived on the second floor; she was married to Sr. Ramos. They had a daughter who was younger than I, and two servants. Yet another brother, who was married to a lady called Dona Carolina lived on the third floor, and they had a baby, though I don't remember whether it was a boy or a girl. The lady very much wanted me to go to her house and hold the baby. She had two servants.

Another brother of this same family lived in another house on the other side of the street a little further down. This house was on the corner made by this road and another one, to the left, and it was there that the entrance was. On the ground floor there was a large room which they called the granary, where they had huge chests full of cereals and vegetables. Behind there were offices where the men worked. This third brother lived on the floor above, and he too was married. The wife's niece lived with them and she was more or less as tall as myself.

I played with her quite a bit and also with Dona Elvira's daughter, in the patio behind the building I have just described. This patio had a cement floor, with steps and some trees, [and was] a very nice place for children to play. We used to take Dona Carolina's baby there with us and it seemed to enjoy itself seeing us all round it and making a fuss of it, while at the same time it could enjoy the lovely fresh air that one could breathe in there.

After a few days – I forget how many – my uncle came to fetch me. While I was there, I slept in a room with a window that looked out onto the road, over the shoe shop. There, as in my uncle and aunt's house, Dona Amelia used to tell one of the maids to bring me my breakfast in bed and to rest on until later in the morning. The ladies asked my uncle if I could stay a few days longer, but my uncle said no it wasn't possible.

Yet another family then appeared, who also wanted me to visit their house. My uncle said I could go, but only for a day otherwise, he said, they cling onto her and never let her go. I don't remember the name of this family. They said that they were the *Condes* (Counts) of Leiria, or belonged to the family of the *Condes* of Leiria, I don't quite remember which. They lived in a large house that looked like a palace, almost at the edge of the city, on the left as you went in the direction of the Patrício family. A lady and two gentlemen lived there, and they had with them a niece whom they were educating and guiding in her studies. The lady asked my uncle and aunt whether my parents would allow me to live with them so that I, too, could study and be educated together with their niece. My uncle replied that he did not think it would be possible, as he had already wanted me to come and live with them in Leiria, and my father would not agree to it. I did not sleep there. In the evening, my uncle came to collect me.

There was yet another family that asked if I could visit their house. They lived in the same street as the Patrício family, but on the right-hand side as you go towards the Cathedral, shortly before you get to the square in front of the Cathedral.

On the ground floor lived a lady known as the «Spaniard»; she had a little grocery shop from which she made just enough to live on from day to day.

Over the shop lived a family, a gentleman with two young daughters, one of whom was already married to a doctor. This doctor examined me very carefully – perhaps at the request of my uncle and aunt, I don't know. He said that I was not ill, but showed signs of exhaustion and weakness which, however, could be remedied by rest and good food. The master of the house took me to a room to show me his workshop, where he had some machines with tall frames, like our looms. He showed me how they worked, but I don't remember what it was he did. I did not sleep there. My uncle came to collect me at the end of the day.

I don't remember how long I had been with my aunt and uncle when my father came to fetch me. We made the journey there and back on horseback.

I returned feeling much better and looking much better in health. My mother, too, had been able to rest a bit because she used to tell the people who called that I was in Leiria, and that if they wanted to speak to me they would have to go there; but it was a long way and there were not, then, any of the means of transport that are available nowadays, so they gave up and went away without insisting on hanging around waiting to see me, bothering my mother with questions and taking up the time that she needed to get on with her housework.

55. Suffering on account of the illness of Francisco and Jacinta

Meanwhile, the conditions of both Francisco and Jacinta had deteriorated considerably, so much so that it seemed likely that it would not be long before they left this earth for Heaven. My mother suffered a great deal on this account because, in addition to being her nephew and niece, she loved them almost as if they were her own children. To a considerable extent they had been brought up and educated by her, as whenever their mother, Aunt Olimpia, needed to go anywhere, to the fields, or to market, or to Vila Nova de Ourém, etc., she used to come and leave them in our house in the care of my mother. This was because, although she had two older daughters, the older one, Florinda, was the one who had to go and look after the sheep, and Teresa was still quite small, not yet old enough to look after her even smaller brother and sister. Thus it was that they grew up to a considerable extent alongside myself, who must have been about a year old when Francisco was born, and three years old when Jacinta was born. And that was how they came to be so fond of me, to the point of not being able to live without me, and my mother was like a second mother to them.

56. In Rev. Fr Vicar's House

I think it was round about this time that Rev. Fr Vicar of Olival sent a message to my mother to ask if she would allow me to spend a few days in his house, saying that I would be company for a sister of his who lived with him.

At the time, I believed this to be the case. Now, however, it seems to me that the reason for the request was rather different, namely, to afford Rev. Fr Vicar a better opportunity to study the events that had taken place, and to observe my own behaviour more closely. In this way, he would be able to speak to me at length, etc., and so form a judgement that was as sure and certain as possible. All this seems to me to have been a good thing, because before they pronounce judgement, those in authority must make certain of the truth.

The person whom Father Vicar sent to Aljustrel to collect me was Senhora Emília of Soutaria. As she and the Vicar were trustworthy people, my parents allowed me to go, saying that it would be good for me to go away for a few days from time to time in order to get a break from the bustle of people all round me, and so avoid becoming ill again.

Senhora Emília came to Aljustrel to collect me; she planned to sleep that night in her own house in Soutaria and the next day she would come to collect me and take me to the Vicar's house in Olival, where I was to live with his sister for three days. On the fourth day after my departure from Aljustrel, Senhora Emilia was to come and collect me in the afternoon; I would sleep that night in her house, and on the following day she would bring me back home to my parents' house. It was a question of five days in all, including the journey there and back, which gave enough time for a bit of a rest.

During my stay there, I only remember a priest who lived with his mother and I think two sisters. He asked for me to go to his house, but I don't remember his name.

57. Yet another scheme for me to study and be educated

Another person who appeared in our house one day was Dr Formigão. He was accompanied by a lady from Lisbon, Dona Assunção Avelar, who wanted to ask my parents if they would allow me to go to her house in Lisbon, so that she could educate me and I could study. [She said] that she would undertake to provide me with everything that I needed, and that I would be well looked after. Dr Formigão introduced the lady, saying that he knew her well, that she was a responsible person, and that she was good and to be trusted.

In reply, my mother said that she herself would be inclined to agree to the proposal and that she would be even be glad of it, [as then she could see] whether, if I were to go away, the whole business would come to an end. However, if the idea was that I was to stay away always, she did not know what my father would say as, on other similar occasions in the past, he had never allowed me to go away for more than a few days at a time.

In spite of this reply on the part of my mother, Dr Formigão asked to speak to my father, perhaps in the hope that he might succeed in persuading him. But my father stuck to what he had said on previous occasions, [namely that] he would allow me to go for a few days in order to rest, but not to stay away for always. Since to go there just for a few days was not what the lady wanted, they went away and nothing came of it.

Afterwards, my mother said to my father:

"It's a pity you feel like that about it. Who knows, if she were to go there and stay there, maybe all this business would come to an end!"

My father replied:

"Maybe so, but at the same time we can't hand over a child of ours who is still so young just like that without knowing what might be the outcome."

To which my mother replied :

"That, too, is true."

And so she continued to carry her cross as best she could, struggling with it up her Calvary.

58. Important visitors

Among the many other people who came and went, a group of ladies appeared, accompanied, I think, by two gentlemen. One of the ladies was already quite old. She sat down – perhaps for the first time in her life – on such a poor pinewood chair, which was all we had. (I have one like it in my cell now which is why I am so fond of it.) They greeted us, asked their questions and then, very politely, took their leave.

The lady who seemed to me to be the oldest was wearing a black satin dress, which was very tight at the hips and from the waist upwards, with long and pointed but very narrow shoes. She was very large, and it was clear that she could only move with difficulty. She went down the steps leading up to our house from the road supported on either side by the two gentlemen, and she walked on up the road leaning on the arm of one of them. My mother and I stood on the steps watching them until they disappeared round the corner. Then my mother turned to me and said:

"These must be some of the people who were rich in the King's time but now, because the Republicans have taken all their money, that lady must not have enough money to buy an extra metre of material to give herself a bit more room in her dress. Poor things!"

Then I was sorry, and I said:

"They may even have been hungry, we could have given them some bread and cheese."

My mother replied:

"We could have, but I never thought of it. But they've gone too far now; let them go!"

I used to pray for that group of people, believing them to be poor until, later on, I heard people saying that the lady was the Baroness (or Marchioness, I'm not sure which) of Pombal, a descendant of the Marquês de Pombal's family.

59. The death of Francisco, and of Lucia's father

While life went on in this way for me, Francisco and Jacinta were becoming increasingly ill until Francisco left this earth for Heaven on 4th April, 1919.

My mother was deeply affected by his death, though at the time she had no idea that three months later, the Lord would ask an even greater sacrifice of her: the sudden death of my father, whom God called to himself in the space of 24 hours on 31st July of the same year, 1919. I will not dwell here on the details of his death, as I have already described it in the Fifth Memoir.

My mother endured this trial with great resignation and acceptance of God's will, saying: "I don't know what else God wants to take from me, but may He give me the grace to give Him everything He asks of me."

Shortly after my father's death, my mother wanted to portion out the inheritance so that my two married sisters could take their share. This apportioning was done with great peace and harmony, thanks be to God. Everyone expressed themselves satisfied with their share. As a result of this share-out, and also as a consequence of the loss of my father's share in the yield from Godmother Teresa's crops – my father was the one who used to till her land – our income was even further reduced.

However, thanks to the great gifts of management and thrift with which God had endowed my mother, she managed, by dint of hard work, to extract from the lands that remained to us enough to keep the family going, so that we never lacked what was necessary, and there was still something over to give to the poor who came knocking at our door. She used to say:

"Whoever has little gives much when they give from the little that they have."

How fitting it would have been for my mother to sing Psalm 32 if she had known it :

> From the heavens the Lord looks forth,
> he sees all the children of men.
> From the place where he dwells, he gazes.
> on all the dwellers on the earth,
> he who shapes the hearts of them all
> and considers all their deeds." [Ps 32, vv 13-15].

60. Lucia goes to Valado to rest

Some ladies from Lisbon who owned a property in Valado invited my mother to spend a few days there with me. They were Dona Guilhermina, who was married to a gentleman whose name I can't remember, and Dona Dolores, who was single; her surname was O'Neill. The married couple had no children.

My mother accepted the invitation so that we could both get a bit of a rest from the constant coming and going of people pestering us with their unending stream of tiring and importunate questions.

The ladies in question received us with great delight and respect, and treated us in the best possible way even taking us, one afternoon, for an outing to the beach at Nazaré, which my mother had never seen. I had, because Godmother Teresa and Godfather Anastácio used to go there for a few days once a year, and they used to take me with them when I was smaller, in the days before I began to look after the sheep. We were the guests of some ladies who may have belonged to the O'Neill family or were just friends,

I'm not sure which. We went to the top of the hill first and said the Rosary in the chapel of Our Lady of Nazaré. Then we went to the cave where the little image is venerated, and where people say that it appeared to the horseman who was about to throw himself into the sea, as one sees from the great commemorative statue in which the horse is holding its front hooves out over the sea. From there we went down to the beach and we went to the home of the family I have already mentioned. Their house was facing the sea, on the far side of the road leading to the quayside. It had some magnificent views, from which one saw steamships, as well as large and small boats rowing across the tossing waves; [we also saw] the fishermen drawing in their nets full of fish and the fishwives shouting noisily to one another as they filled their fish baskets, placed them on their heads, and ran off in different directions. Seeing and hearing all this, I said:

"The women in my village don't shout like that".

Behind the house there was a chapel where the fishermen used to go to hear Mass on Sundays and Holidays of Obligation.

We had supper with the family and then returned to Valado quite late in the evening.

61. Visit to the Monastery of Alcobaça

The next day, Dona Guilhermina's husband invited us to accompany him on another trip. Dona Guilhermina and my mother were feeling tired. So Dona Dolores went with me and the gentleman. He took us to a church, which I imagine must have been the parish church, in order to place on Our Lady's altar a huge sheaf of lovely rosebuds which he had cut in the garden in front of his house. I don't remember under which title that particular statue of Our Lady was honoured. From there, he took us to a see an old uninhabited monastery, where there was a mill driven by the waters of a small river that ran below the monastery, and that was where the monks used to grind the grain to make flour for the bread; there, too, they caught the fish that they ate. That is what we were told. We saw the monastery both outside and inside, the cells, the kitchen, the refectory, the choir, the church, etc. and we returned to Valado in time for our meal.

I don't remember whether it was on that day that a priest came to supper – I presume at the invitation of the family. He may have been the local parish priest, and during supper he asked me quite a few questions.

I also don't remember how many days we spent there before returning to Aljustrel. We were very sorry to go. The gentleman and the ladies wanted us to promise that we would return there for a few days' rest every year.

They amused themselves quite a bit with me, wanting me to sing our regional songs. My mother, too, sang and danced some of them with me.

Recently, I was told that [the Venerable] Jacinta Marto had been there too. I don't remember her being there on that particular occasion; maybe she went some other time, I don't know.

162. Invitation to Lisbon

Dr Formigão came again later on to ask my mother whether, now that my father had died, and as it had been he who had not wanted to let me go to Lisbon the first time, she would now agree to my being entrusted to the care of Dona Assunção Avelar in order to study and be educated.

My mother was in a bit of a quandary, bearing in mind what my father had said about it not being right to hand over such a young child without knowing well the people involved and the terms and conditions of the arrangement.

Then Dr Formigão, who knew that my mother had some ailments that the local doctors did not seem able to cure, suggested to her that she should go to Lisbon to consult the doctors there, taking me with her, and staying in the house of the lady in question. She could stay there as long as necessary, get to know the lady, the situation in the house, the conditions and so on, and then decide either to leave me there or to take me back home with her to Aljustrel.

My mother agreed to this suggestion and asked whether, if she did go, she could bring with her a young girl called Emília, from Ramila, who also had a number of serious ailments for which the local doctors seemed unable to find any remedy.

Dr Formigão said he thought that would be alright, but that he would go to Lisbon to discuss the matter with Dona Assunção Avelar. He would then return to give us her reply and to arrange the date for us to go to Lisbon.

He returned in due course, I don't remember exactly how many days later, saying that the lady would be delighted to receive the three of us into her house and from there we could go as often as necessary to see the doctors. And he fixed with my mother the date we were to go to Lisbon.

My mother informed Emilia's parents of the date and time she was to be at the station in order to travel with us to Lisbon. And when the day came, we went. Dr Formigão's sister travelled with us from Santarém to Lisbon because my mother was not used to travelling or to going to big cities.

On the day arranged, there we were at the station in Chão de Maçãs. We went on horseback. My brother Manuel and my sister Gloria accompanied us, in order to take the horses back to Aljustrel, they having walked there in the first place. Emília, too, arrived on horseback, accompanied by her father.

Here I record an incident connected with another that I have already described, in relation to my visit to Torres Novas, when my mother reprimanded me for my description of the train I had seen when I returned home.

When we reached the station and had bought the tickets, we went out onto the platform to wait for the train to come. I went to the front to look down the track and see [the train] coming. As soon as I saw it, I took hold of my mother's hand and pulled her to the front, saying:

"Now look and see whether I was telling lies or the truth: Look at the chimney belching out smoke, and the little houses trotting along behind it, and all the people inside and looking out the windows, moving along one behind the other with no horses or oxen pulling them along?"

My mother said:

"You're right, child. This time you really did tell the truth. I'm the one who had never seen anything like it."

We then said goodbye to my brother Manuel and my sister Gloria and to Emilia's father, got into the train and off we went.

63. In Dona Assunção Avelar's house

When we got to Lisbon we were met by Dᵃ Assunção Avelar's housekeeper, Joana, and her chauffeur with the car to take us to her house. She welcomed us with great respect, joy and attentiveness.

Dona Assunção Avelar was unmarried, a good Christian and of a noble, monarchical family. She kept the monarchical flag hidden in the altar, folded up underneath the altar stone, in case the Republicans should discover it. She kept herself hidden, too, to some extent, out of fear of the Republicans who at that time were persecuting those who supported the monarchy.

In the house she had a chapel, where the Blessed Sacrament was reserved, and a chaplain went there every day to celebrate Mass. She had five maidservants and one manservant, the chauffeur, who also acted as butler, serving at table in a special uniform. He also used to polish the silver decorations on the walls, the chandeliers in the reception rooms, the brass knobs on the stair banisters, as well as looking after a small garden located behind the house.

Joana, who was the housekeeper, made sure that everyone faithfully carried out the duties assigned to them, that everything was in good order and on time; she also transacted business in the bank, etc.

It was Guilhermina, the lady's personal maid, who looked after the lady of the house, went everywhere with her and was always available in case she should be needed; she also looked after the chapel, the vestments, liturgical linen, and so on. The chapel was next door to the room where the lady of the house slept. Guilhermina also looked after the room where her mistress used to work, read, write and receive the visits of intimate friends. With these she would converse and sometimes they used to amuse themselves by playing games. The lady had three tables with different games. She seemed to like to play cards with me, and was amazed at how good I was at it, nearly always winning. She used also to get me to play with her friends but I have an idea, though I'm not sure, that they used to arrange things so that I would win. They also expressed surprise at the speed with which I sorted the kings and queens etc. after the game. The lady sometimes also played with my mother, and expressed admiration at the way she managed the cards. She also began to teach me how to play the other two games, but I did not get very far; one was dominoes, I don't remember what the other one was called.

The lady was far from well, and used to rest for hours on a small balcony overlooking the garden behind the house on the first floor. She had a heart condition and did not often go out. She, with her entire household, heard Mass every day in her private chapel. She received Communion and used to make her thanksgiving, I don't know exactly for how long, perhaps for a quarter of an hour. Then she took her breakfast, which consisted of tea and toast. Before meals, she used to bless herself and pray, asking God to bless the food that we were going to eat; after the meal she again blessed herself and gave thanks to God. After the evening meal, she used to wait until the staff had finished their tasks. Then they all gathered round her, quietly chatting. After a while, she went with them all to the chapel to say the Rosary, singing a hymn between each decade. The Rosary was followed by the Salve Regina and the Litany; then, asking God and Our Lady to bless everyone, she went off to bed. At that time there was neither radio nor television, thanks be to God.The third servant was the parlour maid. It was her job to clean the reception rooms, shake and sweep the mats and animal skins that were on the floor, and see to the flowers which were placed in long narrow vases, etc. She also looked after the rooms occupied by guests, and it was she who answered the door and ushered visitors into the reception rooms. Depending on who it was and what they wanted, she would inform her mistress, give the reason for their visit, and take back the reply or, alternatively, accompany her mistress, if it was someone who had come to see her. If the callers were intimate friends, she would accompany them to the sitting room where the lady was. Afterwards, she would accompany the visitors out, opening the door for them and bidding them goodbye. She also took care of the clothes, ironing them and placing them in people's rooms, or changing them according to the season, etc. She also looked after the dining room.

The fourth servant was the cook. She was responsible for the kitchen and pantry, for cleaning and tidying the kitchen, washing up the dishes, cleaning the cutlery and putting it away, etc., helped by the other serving maids.

The fifth servant did all the messages. She ran errands, did the shopping, etc., cleaned the stairs, shook out the floor mats, cleaned the stair rods that were used to keep the stair carpet in position, the bathrooms and the entrance hall, and washed all the clothes in a small basement situated at the back of the house, with a door giving onto the garden.

The kitchen, the dining room, the guests' sleeping quarters and the servants' workroom, where they did their manual work such as ironing, etc., were all situated on the ground floor.

The lady's rooms were on the first floor, as were the chapel, the reception rooms, the drawing room with the piano and game tables, as well as sofas and armchairs. This room looked out onto a balcony at the back of the house, with marvellous views over the Tagus, from which you could see ships, the airport and the coming and going of aeroplanes – at that time there were very few as compared with today. For myself, my mother and Emilia, all this was very wonderful, like a dream! And to see it all through binoculars! It was on that balcony that the lady used to rest for hours on end, reading or writing, and at the same time breathing in the fresh air from the Tagus and the wooded areas round about.

The lady was very pious. From time to time she used to get up and make a visit to the Blessed Sacrament, saying:

"Other visitors come and go. This One never goes away, He is always here close to us. We must make sure we ourselves don't go away, leaving Him alone."

And she used to urge the servants to make visits to Him too, saying that it was not a waste of time, rather it was the best-spent time of the day. When she was bidding someone farewell, before going to the drawing room, she used to slip into the chapel for a visit. After the Rosary, she used to pray for the eternal repose of the King and the Prince who had been assassinated, and she used to beg Our Lady's protection for Don Manuel, in the hope that one day he might yet return to his rightful place.

The lady did not want it to be known that I was staying with her, in case people began to call at her house asking to see me and to speak to me. Perhaps it was for this reason that she did not want me to speak to any of the servants other than Joana and Guilhermina; to the others I was only to say "good day" or "good evening" or "God grant us a good night" if I happened to meet them in the passageways or on the stairs. But this was a passing dream. Later, people began to get to know.

64. Sad memories of Jacinta

One day, the lady took myself and my mother to see the house where Jacinta had stayed, the tribune where she had prayed, and the room where she had slept before being admitted to Hospital. There we met Mother Godinho, who already knew me from having seen me in Fatima. From there [the lady] took us to the hospital to see the ward and the bed where Jacinta had died.

Shortly afterwards, the Misses O'Neill from Quinta do Valado, who were friends of hers, happened to call on her; they, too, had already made my acquaintance. When they saw me there, they were surprised and asked if I might spend at least one day in their house. As they were friends, the lady said 'yes', and so I went.

Another day, Dr Eurico Lisboa came. He, too, had met me in Fatima. He asked if he might take me to the beach in Parede, where he was on holiday with his wife and children. The lady said yes and took me there. We also went to see the sanatorium, the house, the wards and the patients who were there in a long gallery to get the benefit of the sea air which was facing them. That's how people got to know where I was.

65. My mother's complaint is diagnosed

In the meantime, my mother and Emilia had been seen by the doctors. In my mother's case, the doctors diagnosed a displaced vertebra in her spine, a displaced kidney and a fairly advanced cardiac lesion. They said that the kidney could be operated on, but they would not guarantee the result, as they did not know whether or not her heart would stand the strain. This being so, my mother decided not to have the operation. They prescribed a corset for her which she hardly ever used as she said that she felt worse wearing the corset than without it. And so she lived for many more years with a certain amount of pain, but able to live her normal life as she had always done. Clearly, as far as healing her was concerned, Our Lady relieved her of the acute pain so that she could go on living a normal life, but did not heal her completely.

The diagnosis of the Lisbon doctors was the same as that made by Dr Carvalho in São Mamede many years earlier.

Emília, too, had kept her various medical appointments, always accompanied by my mother and by Joana, the housekeeper, who had also accompanied my mother. The mistress of the house had very kindly asked her to be responsible for discovering which were the best specialists, making the necessary appointments, and accompanying my mother and Emilia when they went, all of which the housekeeper did with the best will and dedication in the world.

I don't remember exactly what the doctors called Emilia's complaint, but they said it was incurable. They said it was due to the close blood relationship between her parents. They had another son who was an invalid and could only move about in a wheel chair, and their other children were all more or less sickly. They lived in the Ramila area, the second house on the right on the way from Lomba.

In due course, I don't remember how many days later, both my mother and Emilia returned to Fatima, leaving me in Lisbon in the care of Dona Assunção Avelar, who was to educate me and help me to study and also, according to my mother, "to see if, once she has left Fatima, the whole business comes to an end". When they heard my mother say this, Dona Assunção and Dr Formigão laughed, and said:

"Yes, indeed, Senhora Maria Rosa, you are right. It is a good thing to try everything in order to establish the real truth."

My mother was pleased to find that they understood her point of view.

66. People thought that Lucia had disappeared

Meanwhile, my disappearance was causing an outcry in Fatima. My mother refused to say where I was, as Dona Assunção had asked her not to, in case people began to go to her house demanding to see me and talk to me there.

The outcry was such that the authorities summoned my mother to appear before the Administration. She went, and all they wanted to know was where her daughter Lucia was, to which she replied:

"My daughter is where she wishes to be and where I, too, wish her to be. I will not say where she is because I don't want people to begin going there looking for her and wanting to question her and take her away from her studies, as they used to do here in Fatima. She's where she is in order to study and be educated. And I also want to see whether or not, once she has left Fatima, all this affair will come to an end and I can once again live in peace in my house, which I can't do with so many people continually coming and knocking on my door."

"When they heard this reply, they laughed, said I was right and sent me away." I only heard afterwards that they had said this as I was not present at the time.

While this was happening in Fatima, the fact that I was staying in Lisbon was beginning to become known until one day Dona Assunção Avelar was warned that the civil authorities were trying to discover my whereabouts.

The lady was afraid because at that time those who were in favour of the monarchy were still much persecuted and she, being a supporter of the monarchy, was in danger. Moreover, as she was also responsible for me, she feared what might happen to me.

So she got in touch with Dr Formigão and they decided that his sister should come at once to Lisbon to collect me and, if it proved impossible to have me educated in Portugal, she would discuss the matter with a niece of hers who was a Dorothean Sister (her name was Mother Lindim, and she happened to be in Lisbon just then, as superior of a small atelier in S. Marinha) and see whether I could be admitted to the school for Portuguese girls run by the Dorothean Sisters in Tuy, Spain.

67. Lucia goes to Santarém

With these plans in mind, Dr Formigão came immediately to Lisbon to collect me. As soon as he arrived, we left for Santarém, at night, on the first available train.

When we arrived in Santarém, Dr Formigão took me as a guest to his house. His Reverence lived with his mother and sister. I lived there in hiding, without going out or appearing at the windows. Dr Formigão used to go out to celebrate Mass, I don't know in which Church, and used to bring me Communion in the house.

After a few days had passed (I'm not sure how many, perhaps a week), and when it seemed that things had calmed down somewhat in Lisbon, Dr Formigão thought that I could go out on the Sunday, in order to go to Mass in the Church of the Miracle, which was close by. Not many people went there and one got to it by means of a narrow and little-frequented street. So I went there with his mother and sister, but I was at once recognised by a friend of hers, Dona Adelaide, who I think was a sister of the Countess of Margaride.

The back door of her house was opposite the side entrance to the church. One only had to cross the narrow street. When Mass was over, this lady greeted us and when she was told of the reason why I was there, she suggested that I could perhaps do my studies and be educated in a nearby school run by Dona Luisa Andaluz, and she offered to allow me to stay in her house, which would give her great pleasure, and so I would not have far to go to get to school. She took us to see her house, to show us how suitable it would be for me, entering and leaving by the back door.

From there, she took us to Dona Luisa Andaluz's school to see whether I could be admitted to it, and on what terms. When we got there, we entered through a gateway into a small courtyard, then up a flight of outside steps and into a glassed-in gallery.

Dona Luisa appeared at once to greet us, and expressed herself very ready to receive me as a pupil, saying that she would be delighted to do so. We said goodbye to her and went back home. When we got there, Dr Formigão was quite tired of waiting for us to come back so that we could have lunch. When he was told of the reason for our delay, he was pleased, because perhaps that would prove to be the solution to the problem. In that way, I would be close to his house and His Reverence would be able to keep an eye on me and help me spiritually. He said he would go and speak to Dona Assunção Avelar, who might very well agree to the proposal.

However, while all this was being planned in Santarém and Lisbon, it was proving impossible to pacify the people in Fatima who wanted to know where I was. Some people were saying that I ought to be there so that people could see me; others that I ought to be there so that people could talk to me or so that I could answer their questions, etc. and my poor mother, without revealing where I was, continued to suffer – God alone knows how much –on account of all this.

In order to put an end to all the murmuring, Dr Formigão decided that I should make a surprise visit to Fatima and spend a few days there before I went away to school.

With this end in view, I was accompanied to Fatima by Dr Formigão's sister together with an 18 year old girl called Cecilia, who had recently been baptised. I have a feeling that she was later one of the foundresses of the Religious Sisters of Our Lady of Dolours.

68. Meeting with the Bishop of Leiria

Meanwhile the Diocese of Leiria had been restored and Don José Alves Correia da Silva had been consecrated Bishop. As soon as he took possession of his Diocese, he wanted to find out all about the happenings at Fatima, and the whereabouts of the sole survivor of the three little shepherds.

When he heard that I was actually in Fatima at that time, he asked a trustworthy lady to see if she could bring me to Leiria. As soon as she could, this lady, Dona Gilda, came to Aljustrel and asked my mother to allow me to go with her to Leiria because the Bishop wanted to speak to me.

My mother already knew the lady, as she was a friend of my uncle and aunt who lived in Leiria, and a customer of my cousin Laura (who was a dressmaker). So she agreed to let me go, since it was the Bishop who asked for it, even though I had only recently returned to Fatima and people were complaining about my absence. So I went, in the lady's carriage, accompanied by her husband, who drove the horses.

When we got to Leiria, I wanted to go and stay overnight in my uncle and aunt's house, but the lady said no, I was to stay in her house, so that is where we went; it was quite a bit further on, in the street leading to the station.

When we were seated at table eating our supper, the lady asked me if I would like to go with her to the 9 a.m. Mass in the Cathedral the next day, [adding that] it would be celebrated by the Bishop. I said 'yes, I would'. She then asked if I wanted to go to confession before receiving Communion from the Bishop during the Mass. I [again] said 'yes, I would'. "Would I like to go to confession to the Bishop?" I said 'no, I would be [too] embarrassed; I would rather go to confession to some other priest."

The next morning, we went early to the Cathedral. We made our way towards the high altar and saw that there was a priest hearing confessions in the confessional on the left-hand side. We knelt down in the benches in front of the confessional, to wait until the person in front of us had finished. As soon as that person left the confessional, Dona Gilda got up and went to make her confession. I waited until she had finished, and when she left the confessional, I knelt down on the other side to make my confession. When I had finished I went and knelt down beside her. I was very surprised to see the Bishop himself coming out of the confessional. I turned to Dona Gilda and said :

"So it was the Bishop!"

"Yes, it was," she said. "Did you like him ?!

"I did", I replied.

We then went to one of the front benches to assist at the Mass. When the time came, we went up to receive Communion, and when we had made our thanksgiving, we returned home. We had our breakfast and then set off for the Bishop's Palace, where the Bishop received us with the greatest of kindness and courtesy.

After the initial exchange of civilities, Dona Gilda asked leave to withdraw, saying that she would take the opportunity of attending to some business while the Bishop was talking to me. With that, she left the room, closing the door behind her.

69. The Bishop suggests the idea of going to Porto

The Bishop put me sitting on a sofa beside him and began to question me about the apparitions. I replied to his questions to the best of my knowledge and ability. He then asked me if I would like to leave Fatima and go to Porto, to study and be educated in a boarding school. I replied that there was already a lady in Lisbon, who had been a good friend to me, in whose house I had stayed for a time, and that she was arranging for me to go to a boarding school to study and be educated. The Bishop replied that I would be better off in Porto because I needed to be somewhere where I was not known, and that this would not be possible in Lisbon, where I was already well known; that Porto would be better as I was as yet unknown there; that I would not speak about the apparitions in Fatima to anyone, nor about my parents and family, except to give their names, without saying where they lived.

No-one would visit me, except the ladies to whose care he intended to entrust me, so that they could keep an eye on me; that these ladies, too, were very good and would see to it that I lacked nothing; that I was not to write to anyone except my mother but I was to send my letters to the Vicar of Olival, who would be responsible for delivering them to my mother, and that she would do the same with any letters she wrote to me, sending them to the Vicar of Olival to be sent on to me c/o His Lordship; that I would not return to Fatima for the holidays nor for any other purpose without his permission. I said that I would have to ask my mother's permission about all that, and that I did not know whether she would agree because, since she had already promised Dona Assunção that she would allow me to stay with her, I did not know whether or not she would now agree to allow me to go somewhere else. The Bishop then said that he would be responsible for seeking my mother's permission; that I was not to divulge anything of what had been said between us to anyone and that I was to do my best to say nothing more about the apparitions or reply to questions during the rest of my stay in Fatima. I replied that this would be difficult as the people were very insistent and refused to go away until I had given them an answer to their questions.

The Bishop smiled and gave me his blessing, which I received kneeling and kissing his blessed ring. At that point, the Bishop's secretary, Rev. Fr Maia, and Dr Marques dos Santos came to take their leave of the Bishop, the latter wearing his clerical dress consisting of a great cloak and shoes with buckles, which I had never seen before, as the government of the time forbade the wearing of clerical dress and religious habits. [The clergy] wore secular clothes, but with great religious modesty, composure and dignity. They always appeared [in public] in a black suit and clerical collar.

I returned with Dona Gilda to her house, buoyed up with the hope that it was going to be possible for me to live somewhere without being recognised.

The lady allowed me to spend a day with my uncle and aunt and then she and her husband brought me back to Fatima. This lady was married and she lived with her husband and a niece of her husband's who was already engaged to be married. Perhaps it was for this reason that this lady, too, thought to ask my mother to allow me to live in her house, which bordered on the road leading from the town to the station, as a companion to herself and her husband when her niece got married; she said I could study there and she would pay all my expenses.

My mother said this would not be possible as other people had already asked the same thing.

When I returned to Fatima, I carefully kept my secret, but the joy I had felt when I bade farewell to the Bishop did not last long. I began to think of Dona Assunção, whom I was so fond of and who had been so good to me; of my sisters whom I would lose touch with and would not be able to write to. I thought, too, of my uncles and aunts and all my other relatives, of my home where I had spent such an innocent and happy childhood! I thought of Cova da Iria, the Cabeço, Valinhos, the well where we had tasted the delights of Heaven! [To be faced with leaving all that], just like that, for always! And to go I knew not where, to Porto, but I did not even know where Porto was, nor did I know anyone there.

These thoughts and reflections made me so sad that going to Porto seemed to me like being buried alive, and I said to myself: "No, I won't go. I prefer to go to Lisbon or to Santarém. If I am there, I can come back to Fatima from time to time, see my family and keep in touch with them. If I go to Porto, none of this will be possible! No, I won't go! I said 'yes' to the Bishop but now I say that I have changed my mind and I don't want to go there!"

70. With the Vicar of Olival

I don't know how much time passed with me in this state of mind. Then, one day, the parish priest of Fatima told my mother that the Vicar of Olival wanted to talk to her and that she was to go to Olival to see him, taking me with her.

At first, my mother said that she would not go. It was a long way and she had neither the health nor the strength for walking long distances. But afterwards, she began to think that Rev. Fr Vicar would be displeased with her if she did not go, so she decided to undertake the journey after all, [Her plan was] to go in the morning of one day as far as Soutaria, have a rest there and sleep overnight at Dona Emilia's house; then, on the next day, go on to Olival, have her talk with the Vicar and return to Soutaria where she would again stay overnight with Dona Emilia and finally return to Fatima on the following day. By thus taking the journey in easy stages, she thought perhaps she would be able to manage it, and so keep in the Vicar's good books. [She said] she would make this sacrifice for the love of God, and then perhaps God would help her more and better.

So she arranged the day for us to go, and off the two of us went on foot over roads and stony pathways, crossing mountains, fields and silent hills where we heard only the sound of our own voices praying the Rosary: Hail Mary, Holy Mary; pray for us etc.; Our Father who art in Heaven; Thy will be done on earth as it is in heaven etc.; Glory be to the Father and to the Son and to the Holy Spirit etc., as we slipped the beads of the rosary through our fingers.

From time to time we sat down on a stone at the side of the road so that my mother could rest a bit.

At other times, we met one of the people who lived in the place we were passing who knew us from having been to Fatima, and they would come up to us and say:

"Well! Is this where you are, Senhora Maria Rosa? Where are you going? Would you like to come into my house for a bit of a rest?"

To which my mother replied:

"Thank you very much, I want to see if, by stopping overnight in Soutaria, I can get to Olival tomorrow. Rev. Fr Vicar sent for me as he wants to talk to me, so that's where I am going. All for the love of God!"

And on we went, breathing the fresh air of the fields, valleys and hillsides, listening to the chirruping of the birds singing in the treetops and fluttering about in front of us, flying backwards and forwards across the road along which we were walking.

In due course we arrived in Soutaria and knocked on Senhora Emilia's door. It was my mother's first time there, though I knew her well. She came out to see who was knocking and when she saw us she exclaimed with pleasure:

"What is this? Senhora Maria Rosa and Lucia here? Come in, come in, the house is yours! What a shame you did not arrive a little earlier, and you could have had dinner with the others. But it doesn't matter. While you are having a bit of a rest, my maid will prepare something for you to eat."

She was a widow, who lived alone with her maid.

"Come in here and rest in Lucia's bed in Lucia's room."

What she described as 'Lucia's bed' and 'Lucia's room' was where I had slept when I went to Olival. When she asked what we were doing there, my mother replied:

"Rev. Fr Vicar sent a message to say I was to go there as he wants to talk to me."

"But it's a long way to walk for someone of your age and with your complaints. Why did you not come on horseback? I have accommodation here for animals, and the journey wouldn't be so tiring."

"I did think of that," my mother replied, "but going on horseback is very painful for me, and so I prefer to put up with being tired. That's why I thought of coming today, staying here tonight, if you will be so kind as to put us up, and going on tomorrow to Olival, then returning here for another night, after which we will return to Fatima."

"Will I put you up for the night? I shall be delighted, and tomorrow I shall go with you to Olival," Senhora Emilia replied.

The next day, we set off in the morning to walk to Olival. When we got there, Rev. Fr Vicar was not in. He had not yet returned from the church where he had gone to celebrate Mass. His sister sent at once to fetch him. When he came he greeted us warmly and brought us into his study. Senhora Emilia withdrew, saying that she was going shopping and would return later to accompany us back to Soutaria.

Rev. Fr Vicar began by telling my mother that he had summoned her at the behest of the Bishop in order to ask her permission for me to go to Porto instead of returning to Lisbon or Santarém. [I was to be] entrusted to the care of the Bishop, and of a lady whom the Bishop would appoint to be responsible for me, to help me in any way I needed, and to pay all the expenses for my schooling and education.

When my mother heard this, she was clearly very doubtful about it all, and she said:

"This may not be possible because I have already promised a lady in Lisbon that I would allow her to stay with her, and now I dare not say that I am allowing her to go somewhere else instead. I myself spent a few days in that lady's house; she is very good, and both Lucia here and I myself are relieved because I know she will be well looked after. I know no-one in Porto, I don't know where they will be taking her, or how it will turn out."

Rev. Fr Vicar replied to all this, saying that it was precisely because I knew no-one in Porto and no-one in Porto knew me that it was appropriate for me to go there; [he added that] in order not to be recognised I would change my name, I would not say where I came from nor whose daughter I was, nor would I speak about any other member of the family; that only the lady to whose care the Bishop proposed to entrust me, and the superior of the school to which I would be going, would know who I was but nobody else, so that people did not begin going there to look for me, asking to speak to me, disturbing me and taking up the time that I should be devoting to my studies; that this would not be possible in Lisbon, because I was already well known there.

My mother replied saying that everything that Rev. Fr Vicar had said was true but she did not know how she could go and tell Dona Assunção that I was to go somewhere else.

Rev. Fr Vicar told her not to worry about that, as Dr Formigão would take it upon himself to apologise to the lady on her behalf, and the lady would understand that this was the better solution.

My mother said that since it was the Bishop himself who had asked, and if he would assume full responsibility, subject to her right to come and fetch me if, at any time, she should learn that I was not well or not happy, and provided I myself was willing to go, she would agree to the arrangement. And then she added:

"And then we'll see whether, once she leaves Fatima, all this business will come to an end."

Rev. Fr Vicar smiled and turning to me, said:

"And does the little one want to go to Porto or not?"

I replied :

"I would have preferred to go to Lisbon, but in order to do what the His Lordship the Bishop asks, and subject to the conditions outlined by my mother, then I will go to Porto."

71. The moment of departure

Rev. Fr Vicar was pleased with our reply but urged us once again to say nothing to anyone, not even to the rest of the family. He then invited us to go with Dona Emilia, who was already waiting for us outside, to have lunch with himself and his sister. After several refusals on our part and pressure to accept on his, we accepted his invitation. During the meal there was a little more conversation about all the people who were continuing to come to Cova da Iria and Aljustrel. We then made our farewells and set off back to Soutaria, where we stayed that night. The next morning, after the breakfast that Senhora Emilia prepared for us, we said goodbye to her, without realising that we would not be going there again, and set off once more for Aljustrel. As on the outward journey, we slipped the beads of our rosaries through our fingers as we went, and called on the Mother of Heaven: Hail Mary, full of grace etc., asked God for his help: Our Father, who art in Heaven etc., and praised the Holy Trinity: Glory be to the Father and to the Son and to the Holy Spirit etc. We broke off from time and sat down to rest on a suitable stone which we happened to find by the roadside.

During one of those pauses for a rest, my mother asked me was I really content to be going to Porto. I replied that I would have preferred to return to Lisbon, but that since they say that the Bishop represents God, I was prepared to go to Porto in order to do what he wished me to do. But if I should not be happy there, then my mother could come and take me home. And with this idea we cheered each other up.

Then, getting up once more, we proceeded on our way, offering each step to God as so many acts of love. In his book "Exercícios de Perfeição", P. Afonso Rodrigues* tells the story of a hermit whose cell was a long way from the spring and so he had to walk a great distance each day in order to go there and draw water. As he was making his way there one day with his pitcher on his shoulder, he was trying to work out where he might move his cell to in order to be nearer, and not have to go all that distance every day, when he heard a voice behind him counting 1, 2, 3, 4, 5, etc. and so on. He stopped, looked round but saw no-one. He started off again, and

* *Cf. note 7*

the same voice went on counting; he looked behind once more and still could see no-one; and so on a third time. Then the monk stopped and asked out loud:

"Who is that coming behind me and counting?"

And the voice replied :

"I am your Guardian Angel, counting your steps in order to offer them to God."

Then the monk said :

"If that is the case, then, instead of moving my cell nearer to the spring, I will move it further off so that you will have more to offer to God on my behalf."

In the same way, I hope that our Guardian Angel offered our steps to God for the praise of his Glory, and that my mother is now in Heaven enjoying the reward for all those steps that cost her such sacrifice.

When we got to Aljustrel my mother said she felt she had been ground to bits. She had to stay in bed for two days in order to rest and recover her strength. After that, she returned to her normal life.

In the course of the day, she would ask me from time to time:

"Are you down-hearted? Don't you want to go to Porto? We haven't signed anything, you know. If you don't want to go, don't go!"

To which I replied:

"I'd rather go to Lisbon or Santarém, but as the Bishop wants me to go to Porto, I'll offer the sacrifice to Our Lord and I'll go to Porto."

On 13th June, a lady called Dona Filomena Miranda came to our house in Aljustrel. She was a native of Santo Tirso and she told us that the Bishop of Leiria had asked her to go to Fatima to collect me and take me to school in Porto. [She also said] that she would be staying for three days in Leiria before going on to Porto by train on the 16th at 2 p.m.

My mother replied:

"If she is going to spend three days in Leiria, then let her spend those three days here and then, at 2 p.m. on the 16th, I will be with her at the station so that she can travel on with you to Porto.

I warned my mother that it would be a very long walk and she would not be able for it. But she replied :

"Never mind! God will come to my aid! I want to be the one who takes you and goes with you as far as the station."

72. Saying goodbye to the place where I was born

At 2 a.m. on the morning of the 16th, the alarm clock went off, calling us to get ready to set off for Leiria, accompanied by Sr. Manuel Correia, who was going to work there carrying on his back, hung from the handle of the spade, a bag containing some things that my mother had hurriedly got ready for me to take with me.

We set off by the pale light of Our Lady's candle, the moon, passing Cova da Iria on the way, where we stopped to say the Rosary. Then on we went by paths and shortcuts to make the journey shorter, just as St Joseph and Our Lady must have done with the Child on their way to Egypt, crossing the plains and hillsides, the mountains and valleys of Judea in their efforts to remove the Child from the dangers surrounding Him.

Descending the slopes and climbing to the top of the valleys, sitting down now and again so that my mother could rest, [on we went] until we came to the old pine grove belonging to D. Dinis, the Lavrador, where alone one hears the creaking of the old pine trees, shaken by the fresh morning breeze; the noise of the pine cones falling to the ground, the raucous call of the ravens crowing in the treetops; and breathing in the fresh air of the morning breeze, with the sweet scent of the humble flowers of the field, of the eucalyptus trees, of the heather, gorse and rosemary, which seemed to put spirit and life into us. And on the actual road, meeting light carts coming the other way – very few at that early hour – leaving us behind them wiping our eyes from the dust that their passage had stirred up.

73. The old suitcase, an abiding souvenir of my departure

In due course, we arrived in Leiria. Before going to my aunt and uncle's house, my mother wanted to go to a shop and buy a little case for me to take to Porto, in which to put the few things, more suitably arranged, which she still had time to get for me: some underclothes, exercise books and school books, etc.

I still have that case, which has accompanied me throughout my life. It is the one I used to take on holiday to carry my few possessions; I took it to Spain when I went to be a Religious; I used to take it every year to the beach when I went there to bathe on the doctor's orders, I brought it back with me to Portugal when I returned in 1946, and to Carmel when I came here with the permission of my Superiors. It is in that case that I keep a few personal possessions that I treasure. I made a grey cotton cover for it so that it would not get spoilt, and it is the case that I took to Fatima with me on the occasions when I went there. It reminds me of my beloved Mother.

We then went to my uncle and aunt's house, who welcomed us wholeheartedly. My mother rested there a bit; we had lunch with my aunt and uncle, went to Sr. Pinto's house to pay a visit to my sister Carolina who was there at the time looking after a little girl who was sick, and from there we went to Leiria station, accompanied by my cousin Laura and my aunt and uncle. Shortly afterwards, Senhora D. Filomena Miranda appeared to accompany me to Porto, and then the train came in. I said goodbye to my cousin Laura and my uncle and aunt – though I did not know it, it was to be the last time I embraced them in this world. Then I hugged my mother who said to me in spite of her tears:

"Off you go, child, and if you really did see Our Lady, she will look after you. I entrust you to Her. But if you were telling lies, I don't know what will happen to you."

Then, with my hand in that of Senhora D. Filomena, I got into the train and looked out through a window to wave goodbye, while my cousin Laura and my uncle and aunt and my mother responded by waving too with one hand while they wiped away with the other the tears that were streaming down their faces as the train gathered speed leaving behind the trees and the fields, and putting an ever greater distance between us. My mother remained with my uncle and aunt for a few days in order to rest and wait for Sr. Manuel Correia, so that she could go back to Aljustrel with him.

Afterwards, she used to come to Porto to visit me – once a year, I think. During the last year that I spent there, the Bishop of Leiria wanted her to go with me to spend a few days' holiday at his Quinta da Formigueira in Braga. It was there that he confirmed me, much to my mother's delight.

74. *Conversation with the Bishop of Leiria*

I took advantage of the opportunity to ask my mother's permission to become a Religious. She replied:

"Look, daughter, I know nothing about such a life. I will ask the Bishop."

And she went downstairs to look for the Bishop, who was sitting reading on a bench opposite the balcony, under the shade of the trellised vines. As soon as His Excellency saw my mother, he called her over to him and made her sit down on the bench beside him. I was watching from the balcony. I did not hear what they were saying, but when my mother came back, after a long conversation with the Bishop, she was very pleased to be able to say 'yes' to my request, on condition that I agreed to let her know if I was not happy, so that she could come and collect me.

One day when we were all eating together, the Bishop asked my mother:

"Tell me, Senhora Maria Rosa, what have you to say about the apparitions there in Cova da Iria?"

She replied :

"Your Excellency, I don't know what to say to you. It's such a big thing, and we are so unworthy, that it seems to me impossible that it could be true."

Then the Bishop said:

"What you say is true, but don't you know that God gives his grace to those who do not deserve it, as he did to St Paul when he knocked him off his horse in order to transform him from a sinner into an Apostle?"

My mother replied:

"Only in that way".

One afternoon we went on foot to the Bom Jesus and Sameiro. There we said the Rosary and returned in the cool air that was blowing through the Bom Jesus wood. The Bishop said to my mother :

"This is more beautiful than Cova da Iria, isn't it?"

My mother replied :

"But Your Reverence did not know Cova da Iria before the apparitions. The people who go there have ruined everything. In my view, there is nothing lovelier than the Cova as it was beforehand."

And, walking slowly, we arrived at the house owned by Dona Maria da Conceição, who had invited the Bishop and ourselves to have supper with her, and was already on the look out for us. After the meal and a bit of conversation, we returned to the Quinta da Formigueira for the night. This lady, Dona Maria da Conceição, was the one whom the Bishop had asked to assume responsibility for me when I left Fatima. It was she who looked after me, and paid my school fees, which she did very willingly and with the greatest of tact and generosity.

75. "The two of us started to sing"

One afternoon, my mother and I went for a walk in the Quinta in order to take advantage of the freshness of the afternoon air. We came to a quarry situated a little lower down, and made our way to the bottom of it, where we sat down on a stone. My mother asked me did I still remember some of the old songs we used to sing in Fatima. I said I did. Believing that no-one could either see or hear us, the two of us began to sing :

> I love God in Heaven
> And I love Him on earth
> I love the field, the flowers,
> I love the sheep on the hillside.
>
> I am a poor shepherdess
> I always pray to Mary
> In the midst of my flock
> I am the midday sun.
>
> I love God ...
>
> With my little lambs
> I learnt to jump.
> I am the joy of the hillside,
> I am the lily of the valley.
>
> I love God ....

When we came to the end, we heard someone laughing. We looked up and there was the Bishop at the top looking down at us and laughing. We got up in order to go back up and greet His Lordship, but he made a sign to us to stay where we were and he himself came down. When he reached us, he sat down on a stone next to us and told us to go on singing as he enjoyed listening to us. So then we sang some verses in honour of Our Lady:

Chorus

It's true, it's true   (repeat)
Heaven is my home!

Heaven is my home,
I long to be there
And it will be mine, never fear (repeat)
Close to the Mother of God, the beloved.

Heaven is my home
Home of eternal bliss,
There I shall always be happy,
Close to the Mother of God, the beloved.

It's true, it's true! ...

Afterwards, we returned to the house because it was nearly time for supper, which we all partook of in a happy frame of mind. While we were at table, the Bishop said to us:

"You have a lovely voice, Senhora Maria Rosa. If you lived nearer, I would recruit you to sing in the choir."

My mother replied:

"I used to have a good voice. Now it's tired and not nearly as good as it used to be."

The days we were to spend there passed very quickly. The Bishop could not stay any longer as his duty called him elsewhere. So we had to go and, after breakfast, my mother said goodbye to the Bishop, thanking him for his kindness in inviting us to stay there, where we were able to attend Mass and receive Holy Communion every day without even having to go out of doors. Then I and Dona Filomena Miranda went with her to Braga station where she caught the train to Leiria where my aunt and uncle – her brother Manuel – were to meet her, and take her to their house until an opportunity presented itself for her to return to Aljustrel.

76. "The one I worry most about is Lucia"

Naturally, my mother's eyes were swimming in tears when she said goodbye, but at the same time she was grateful and happy to have been allowed to spend those lovely few days with me, a privilege she never tired of thanking the Bishop for. Oh! She was after all a mother! And the kind of mother who knew how to fulfil all her duties to the point of giving her life, if need be, for each one of the children whom the Lord had entrusted to her. I remember that 13th October when she said to my father:

"If our daughter is going to be killed, let us go and be killed alongside her."

And without thinking about herself but only about accompanying me, she left the house in that torrential rain and wind to confront the danger unafraid.

I also remember another day when the Bishop asked her:

"How many children did God give you, Senhora Maria Rosa?"

"God gave me seven children," she replied. "One is already in Heaven praying for us. The other six, one boy and five girls are all alive and well, thanks be to God. What's more, they are good children, though not as good as I would like them to be. The one I worry most about is Lucia here, because I am still not absolutely sure that Our Lady really did appear to her."

This was the doubt that tortured her, perhaps to the very end of her life.

When I returned from the station with Dona Filomena to have lunch with the Bishop and take our own leave of him, His Excellency asked me had my mother got off all right. I replied that she had, only she had, of course, been crying. The Bishop said:

"You must thank God for giving you such a good and holy mother. I really enjoyed the few days I spent in her company."

At the time I had not understood, but now, looking back, I have no doubt that the Bishop had wanted me to go to Porto, and not to Lisbon, so that he personally would be in a better position to study the happenings in Fatima, and have a better basis on which to form a judgement and make a pronouncement. That was why [he wanted] to keep me under his jurisdiction, entrusted to the care of trustworthy people who would keep him informed about everything concerning me, and where he himself could keep an eye on me and speak to me whenever he wished, and so be better able to form a balanced judgement about what had happened.

It seems to me that the Bishop acted prudently and that he was guided by the Holy Spirit. Hence, I am deeply grateful to God, to Our Lady, and to the Bishop.

77. "Till we meet in Heaven"

My mother visited me once more, this time going as far as Tuy, in Spain, in order to be present when I made perpetual profession of my vows, on 3rd October, 1934.

After the ceremony, when I at last managed to disentangle myself from all the people who had come to be there, I was able to spend a few moments alone with my mother. [During that time] I said to her:

"You said that you would let me go in order to see whether, once I had gone away, the whole story would come to an end. It is thirteen years now since I left and I have never been back. So has it all come to an end?"

My mother replied:

"Not a bit of it! It just gets worse and worse!".

"So you see, I'm not there now to deceive people: it's God and Our Lady who are there!"

To which my mother replied:

"If I could be quite sure that it was Our Lady who appeared to you, than I would be only too glad to give her the Cova da Iria and everything else that I have. But I'm not sure!"

With that we hugged each other and bade each other farewell until we meet in Heaven!

With the passing of the years, the work she did, and her advancing age, my mother's health began to deteriorate until, one day, feeling that the end of her earthly sojourn was approaching, she wrote me a letter to ask whether, since she could no longer come and see me, I would go and embrace her for the last time, as she did not want to die without seeing me once again.

I showed her letter to my superiors who, in spite of the fact that I belonged to a Congregation of active Sisters, told me that such a thing was out of the question, and that I was to write to my mother and urge her to offer the sacrifice [of not seeing me] to God.

I wrote to the Bishop of Leiria to tell him what had happened. His Excellency's reply was on the same lines, adding that he had already arranged for a priest from the Shrine to go and see my mother and see that she had everything she needed; that she was well looked after, and that my sisters were surrounding her with love, devotion and affection.

Faced with this reply, and seeing in it God's will, I wrote to my mother, urging her to offer her sacrifice to God and telling her that I, too, was offering mine for her and asking God to alleviate her sufferings.

When my mother received my letter, she said:

"So they won't let her return to Fatima even to be present at my death! If I had known that that's how it would be, I would never have let her go there! However, I'll offer this great sacrifice to God so that He will keep her in his care and help her always to be good."

Crying, she bowed her head, resting it in her hands which were supported by her knees.

Some days later, I'm not sure how many, sensing that her end was near, she asked my sister Teresa to book a call through, so that she could at least say farewell to me by phone. My sister helped her to the phone, so that there would be no delay when the call came through. Then she phoned and said what she wanted: that Sr. Lucia be called to the phone to say farewell to her mother who was very ill, close to death in fact, and who was asking to be allowed to say farewell to her daughter by phone, and hear her voice for the last time, as there was no other way. What was my poor sister's dismay when the reply to her request was "no", adding that this too could not be allowed.

My sister had no way of concealing this further refusal from my mother, because she was there beside her, waiting to stretch out her hand and take hold of the receiver in order to say her last farewell to me on this earth.

When my mother heard this further refusal, she said between sobs:

"This is the last drop the Lord kept for me at the bottom of the chalice and which I had yet to drink on earth. I'll drink it for love of Him."

Some days later, during which she savoured all the bitterness of that last drop for the love of God, she asked to be moved to her Lucia's room, as it was there that she wished to live out the rest of her exile. A priest from the Shrine went to the house to bring her the apostolic blessing with a plenary indulgence at the hour of death – it was in those terms that such blessings were given in those days – and she left this earth for Heaven on 16th July, 1942, the Feast of Our Lady of Mount Carmel, to whom she had always had such great devotion and whose scapular she wore. May her soul rest in peace.

At the time, my superiors kept these last two details from me. I only learnt of them much later on when my sister Teresa paid me a visit and told me about them. Even then, we both shed tears and offered them to God for the eternal rest of our mother, in the belief that God had received her into his loving Fatherly arms in order to take her to Heaven to receive the reward of all that she had done for Him and for her neighbour during her life on earth.

So I now pray and sing with the Psalmist:

"Still bearing fruit when they are old, still full of sap, still green, to proclaim that the Lord is just. In him, my rock, there is no wrong." (Psalm 91)

And, as the Bishop of Leiria said to me: "You must thank God for giving you such a good and holy mother."

Yes, I thank God for the good and holy mother He gave me, while at the same time I mourn bitterly over so many others who deliver their children to death even before they are born. "Thou shalt not kill", is what we are told in God's Law (Ex. 20, 13).

I am the last of the seven children that God gave to my parents; if that had been their attitude, I would not be here today.

79. Words of Appreciation

Dr Formigão wrote of my mother as follows: "[She was a] typical Christian woman and a good housewife, devoted to her household tasks; she always endeavoured to instil into her children the holy fear of God and to persuade them to fulfil all their moral and religious duties. She was deeply disturbed by the events that turned the eyes of thousands of people to her humble home, which had hitherto been utterly ignored by the world, and her spirit was torn between the hope that her daughter really had been privileged to see the Blessed Virgin, and the fear that she was the victim of a hallucination that was causing her annoyance, and covering the whole family with ridicule". (Doc. Crit. pp 52-53).

The parish priest of Fatima wrote : "As soon as people began to say that Our Lady had appeared on 13th May to the three children and I heard about it, which would have been about a fortnight later, I sent a message to summon Lucia's mother to come and see me in the parochial residence, and to bring her daughter with her. The mother came with the child, but she was very upset because, she said, she believed the whole thing to be a lie. She ordered the child to contradict what she had said, as such a lie was very wicked. She threatened, and said she had already threatened, her daughter that all sorts of things would happen to her if she persisted in saying that she had seen Our Lady when it wasn't true. She said that only to her did such things happen.. etc., etc.. I tried to calm the poor mother down, saying that if what people were saying was true, it was a great glory for her and for her family. "Oh! If only it were true... but if it is a lie?!" the doubting mother exclaimed.

I advised her to continue to look after her daughter as she had done up to that moment. When the time came for the girl to go back to the place of the Apparition, she was neither to tell her to go nor prevent her from going, but to bring her to me, on her own, on the day after the Apparition if the girl should continue to say that she had been given the grace of seeing Our Lady [again]. All this the mother promised to do; she even offered to bring her daughter to see me on the evening before the Apparition, or the evening before that, so that I could tell her what, or what not, to do, or say, at the time of the Apparition. I counselled her against this, in order to avoid provoking any criticism on the part of impious or evil-minded people, as in fact happened." (Doc. Crit., pp. 254-255).

In this, I believe that my mother was led by the Holy Spirit, who instilled in her from the very beginning the desire to entrust her daughter, with the Message of which she was the bearer, to the direction of the Church; and this she was able to do when she entrusted me to the fatherly pastoral care of His Excellency D. José Bishop of Leiria, a charge which His Excellency carried out with tactful care, when he assumed responsibility for the poor little lamb which the Lord had entrusted to his pastoral care, in order to direct its steps to greener fields and pastures, and allow it to drink from the waters of salvation.

Steps which Holy Church supervised, desirous of protecting her from the roaring of the storms raging around her and from the raging waves of the ocean spread out before her.

And so I pray and sing with the psalmist:

"I give God thanks in the land of my captivity,
He has shown his power and majesty to a nation of sinners.
Turn back, you sinners, and do right before him;
who knows if He will accept you and have mercy on you?
I exalt my God; my soul exalts the King of heaven,
and will rejoice in his majesty.
Give thanks worthily to the Lord,
and proclaim his wonders to the nations." (Tob. 13, 8-10).

Coimbra, 25th March, 1993.

The Santos family home in Aljustrel
where Lucia was born and lived until she was 14.

The yard outside Lucia's house with the fig trees in the foreground.

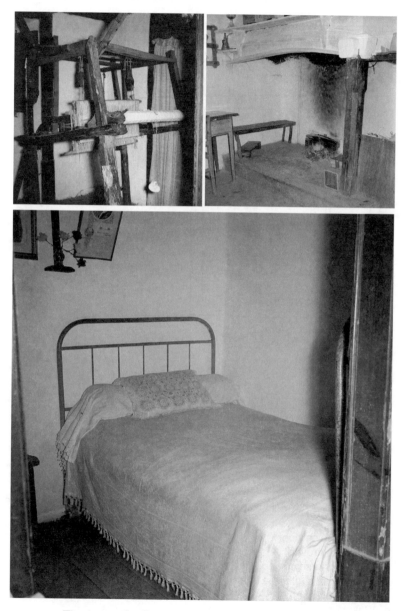

The loom, the fireplace and the Parents' bedroom

Plan showing layout of Lucia's home

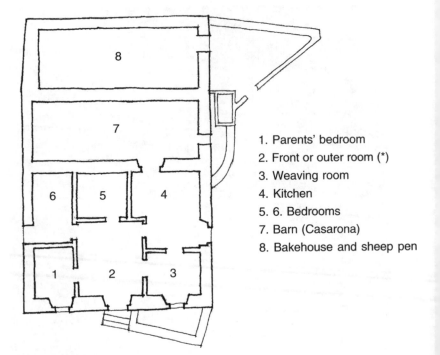

1. Parents' bedroom
2. Front or outer room (*)
3. Weaving room
4. Kitchen
5. 6. Bedrooms
7. Barn (Casarona)
8. Bakehouse and sheep pen

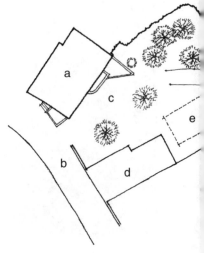

a. Lucia's family home
b. Street
c. Yard
d. Shed where the donkey and oxen were kept
e. Old threshing floor (since destroyed)
f. Existing threshing floor, built several years after the death of Sr. Lucia's father
g. Well where the angel appeared.

(*) (Note: This was the best room in the house, where visitors such as the parish priest, the doctor, etc. were received. It was here that grace after meals and the family Rosary were said. Here, too, all those who came looking for Lucia after the apparitions were received and waited, often for hours, for her to return from pasturing the sheep, etc.

Plan showing general layout of the property

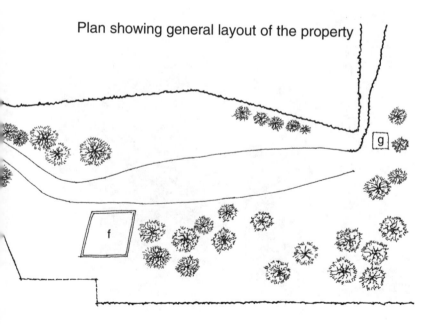

Lucia at the ages of 13, 14, 17 and 74

Maria Rosa with her family in 1920: (back row) Manuel, Maria dos Anjos (with her daughter Gloria), Carolina, Gloria; (front row) Maria Rosa (Lucia's mother, seated), Lucia. (Inset) Maria Rosa

Lucia's brother and sisters in 1968; (from left to right): Gloria (seated), Manuel, Maria dos Anjos, Carolina, Teresa (seated, right);
(Inset) Lucia's meeting with Maria dos Anjos and Carolina in Fatima, in 1981.

*Sister Lucia visits the well and points out the place
where the Angel appeared (Loca do Cabeço)*

CONTENTS

EDITOR'S PREFACE 5

FIFTH MEMOIR

Introduction 7

  1. Prologue 8
  2. Before the Apparitions 9
  3. During the Apparitions 28
  4. After the Apparitions 33

APPENDIX TO THE FIFTH MEMOIR 38

SIXTH MEMOIR

Introduction 45

My father's house, the land where I was born 46

  1. Prologue 47
  2. The Ferreira Rosa Family 51
  3. Maria Rosa: from birth to marriage 54
  4. Unbounded charity 61
  5. Children, grandchildren and great-grandchildren 62
  6. Faithful to her promises 68
  7. Food 70
  8. Motherly care 71
  9. In defence of life 72
  10. More about food 72
  11. Lucia gets up to mischief 74
  12. The Paschal Visit 78
  13. Fruit trees 79
  14. Lucia up to mischief again 81
  15. Caring for our clothes 83

16. The virtuous woman 88
17. Christian charity 90
18. Popular songs 96
19. A lesson for a lifetime 98
20. Paying the price of curiosity 100
21. Another act of Christian charity 102
22. A life of prayer 104
23. "They all want to perch on the roost." 107
24. Household tasks 108
25. The story of the fox 110
26. The fruits of the Holy Spirit 112
27. Sunday afternoons 113
28. Calvary 116
29. Our house began to be much less lively 118
30. The Story of a Princess 119
31. The gift of life 122
32. From the festival to the desert 125
33. Apparitions are children's tales 128
34. The family property at Cova da Iria 129
35. The crops from the Cova are destroyed 130
36. At night, when the visitors had gone 131
37. More and more people 132
38. My father's place of refuge 133
39. My father: a prudent man 134
40. "Perhaps they'll get her to admit that she lied" 137
41. Clarifications 141
42. My father: a peaceable man 143
43. My mother's incredulity 145
44. Hard times 147
45. Confidence in God and sharing 148
46. Poor, humble way of life 149
47. 13th October: doubts persist 150
48. "I am dying with you stuck in my heart!" 151
49. "I already feel better, thank God" 152
50. Supper and thanksgiving 154

51. "There's no way out of this!" 156
52. "Man, let her go, she'll be all right." 157
53. "Little houses, trotting along one behind the other" 158
54. A few days in Reixida and Leiria 159
55. Suffering on account of the illness
    of Francisco and Jacinta 163
56. In Rev. Fr Vicar's House 163
57. Yet another scheme for me to study
    and be educated 164
58. Important visitors 165
59. The death of Francisco, and of Lucia's father 166
60. Lucia goes to Valado to rest 167
61. Visit to the Monastery of Alcobaça 168
62. Invitation to Lisbon 169
63. In Dona Assunção Avelar's house 170
64. Sad memories of Jacinta 173
65. My mother's complaint is diagnosed 174
66. People thought that Lucia had disappeared 175
67. Lucia goes to Santarém 176
68. Meeting with the Bishop of Leiria 178
69. The Bishop suggests the idea of going to Porto 179
70. With the Vicar of Olival 181
71. The moment of departure 184
72. Saying goodbye to the place where I was born 186
73. The old suitcase, an abiding souvenir of my departure . 187
74. Conversation with the Bishop of Leiria 188
75. "The two of us started to sing" 190
76. "The one I worry most about is Lucia" 191
77. "Till we meet in Heaven" 192
78. She left this earth for Heaven" 194
79. Words of Appreciation 195

Execução Gráfica
Gráfica Almondina
Maio 2006